O MOTHER

McSWEENEY'S
SAN FRANCISCO

Cover illustration by Zachary Hobbs

ISBN 978-1-963270-48-8

10 9 8 7 6 5 4 3 2 1

www.mcsweeneys.net

Printed in Canada

O MOTHER

EMERSON WHITNEY

McSWEENEY'S
SAN FRANCISCO

For Grammy

O mother

what have I left out

O mother

what have I forgotten

O mother

farewell

—Allen Ginsberg, *Kaddish and Other Poems*

I felt every move you made even if I was far away. Let me make a portrait of you, looking like a leaf in someone's hand, someone holding it by the stem and walking. Your cheeks rise for laughter often and something like youth haloes you. You put your hair behind your ears, and I'd feel it.

I was in love with you like a dog falling asleep in the living room, soft and public. Everyone could see how much I cared. My care for you and yours for me were sometimes mismatched, but it wasn't your fault. You were so thrown by everything. A car would drive by and you'd get in it. This is part of what made you beautiful.

* * *

I was on my way to your place to be alone with you for the first time since childhood, really. As I drove, I tried to stop rehearsing saying hi to you in my head. Hi, Mom. I was practicing lower octaves for no reason. I was excited, nervous, my fingers tapping the steering wheel.

I drove along the river with the waterworks buildings on either side of the bank, the ones that have large copper roofs and long-dead gold-leaf clocks above the steel doors. They're all missing windows, so they whistle. If you were still here, we'd go back up there this week or over to Marden's to get the tarps they're selling for six dollars each, I think they just liquidated a Lowes. You'd be excited by the new barbecue place over there too, it's the kind with metal trays.

I was driving past the combo mini-golf / go-kart place with the tire track steaming in summer chaos, past that gun range with enormous ARs in silhouette hanging on the building and the handful of purple fireworks stores that are always one hundred percent empty, and I was flirting with moving back to the island. Everything about the idea felt good. We didn't say this kind of thing to each other at the time, but if we had, I would have said something about how the idea of returning felt good on my nervous system.

Do you remember wanting me to live here so badly? Your ask used to live in everything you said.

The heat was gumming up my steering wheel by the time I'd made it Downeast, a seven-hour drive from New York City, and all my cupholders were full of empty coffees. A pink light moved into the car with me from a neon car-wash sign nearby.

When I pulled up, you were hanging out of the back door of a thin-walled warehouse on the edge of town, holding the glass door open with your foot and waving a red shirt. Honey, look, you were saying. My heart was ignited. Just seeing you had the capacity to make me so happy. What is that?

You were showing me that you'd patched the elbows of my favorite flannel. I pushed out of the car and into your hug. You were smiling so big and you smelled like apples. Your glasses were high up on your nose. I fixed it for you! you said. Honey! Hi! I can't close the door or it'll lock! Your hand was small on my back.

Oh wow, Mom! I love this, I said, taking the flannel from you. Damn, are we Gilmore Girls now?

Neither of us had ever watched a full episode of *Gilmore Girls*, so my joke rattled around on the floor like out of batteries. It was the kind of thing I'd say to make friends laugh. I was performing for an imagined audience. You were too, I could tell your tone was for your boss, Willie, or whoever else was inside. I was twenty-two and you were forty-four.

* * *

In that warehouse, we were saying hello and I was running my hand along the things in there: the ceramic palm tree and ceramic wicker basket, the carousel horses—this one's scary, you'd said of it, interrupting yourself. You felt everything you saw. The horse's open mouth showed big pink wooden gums. You'd been telling me about how you were almost finished cleaning, just give me another forty-five minutes or so, you were saying.

Marrrrie, Willie sang. He was your boss bursting into the room. Look at this! He mazed through antiques toward us with this giant painting of a chickadee like a sail.

It's huge! he said. He was talking loud, jutting his hip.

What do you think of this for the living room of Fox Run? he asked and angled it toward you.

Love it! you said, whirling around toward me.

A spotlight landed.

What do you think about it, Em? You beamed.

What do I think? I pointed at myself.

It's you??! Willie said. I almost didn't recognize you—so butch!

That makes sense, I said.

I'd been on the island visiting my grandparents the year before and had weeded for him and his landscaping business under tangled pines. I'd had longer hair. He ran the business with his longtime boyfriend and, as queers, we'd become sort of friends. I hadn't seen you that summer because you were in rehab. This was your first summer sober in my lifetime.

You brushed back a strand of hair that had fallen out of your ponytail. You were smiling. We had a similar inner hum.

Just give me a few minutes, my honey, you'd said. We're wrapping up around here. You turned toward a vacuum.

A Jeep Wrangler pulled up really close to the front door, Willie looked at it over my head. Brian and Shawn... he said, turning to me. Want to run some errands with us while you wait for your mom? We could go to Beech Hill Pond?

I looked over at you and you looked up at me with your foot on the pedal to lean the vacuum back. This was half a second but your eyes looked pulled behind your glasses. The skin on your face by your ears seemed to pinch. Oh, would you rather I don't go? I said because your face was pleading. Would that be easier?

I put my hands out. I don't need to go anywhere. My shoulders went up to my ears and I leaned on a decorative trunk by the door to show I wasn't leaving. Willie slunk out. I knew the trunk was decorative because it crunched when I leaned back.

I think I'm just hungry, actually, I said, regretting saying it immediately. The door closed behind Willie. You turned to me with glacial eyes, brown under the blue. I was so accustomed to this look, an exhausted one that could grow and grow.

All I've eaten today is gum, you said and turned back to your vacuum.

Okay, what can I do? I took my hands out of my pockets. Want me to go get us some food?

No, honey, you said. There's nothing you need to do. Just keep me company. I made us dinner, it's in the fridge just ready to heat up. Can you wait for it? I made it so nice.

Of course, I said, and picked up a dust cloth from a nearby table and started wiping down a mirror next to me for no reason. My reflection flashed back in weird waves. You vacuumed a chevron pattern in the carpet.

I glanced up at the one hanging plant in the corner of this whole place. It was alive, I realized because there was a puddle on the floor underneath it. Someone had been watering it and I guessed it was you.

When you told me you were ready to go, I was very hungry. The linoleum squeaked under us as we walked back toward the door. You pointed to this large night-light in the shape of a goose under the plant. I turn it on for the night, you said, walking over to it. I don't know why. I wish I could bring it home.

Can we? I touched it. It was an open-mouthed goose with a plot of plastic green grass between its legs.

No, honey, we can't do that, you petted its back. Goodnight, warehouse! Goodnight, decor! you said, holding the door open for me.

I love you, my honey, I'm excited for you to be here! We stepped out into the parking lot and I was in a movie about reconnecting with a parent.

The concrete smelled good and it was hazy from the fog, wet headlights were going by. I fumbled my keys out of my pocket, realizing I'd been holding my breath because you were being sweet and real and that felt perilous. I shook my head as if coming up out of water in order to lose the thought.

What am I telling you? I guess it's that usually, it felt like we were more like siblings. Constantly people say "your parents" when talking about my grandparents. Grammy and Grandpa do it too sometimes, saying Dad instead of Grandpa by accident.

Look, your mom is doing great, Grammy and Grandpa had said a few days earlier over the phone, let this visit be just about her. Don't come see us. You guys spend some time together.

You never know, they'd said. Meaning you could die anytime or I could.

* * *

It occurs to me remembering this day that the only times I ever saw you interacting with other people was when I shadowed you at work. It also occurs to me that most families aren't made up of extremely asocial people. Our family is reclusive. How many times have you said that you'd wished Grammy and Grandpa had just one friend. Just one, you'd say and hold up a pointer finger and push it at me. When you'd say this to me, I'd always think, does she not realize I'm feeling the same about her?

I wondered often what it would have been like to have a parent who had friends that were other parents. There'd be a social net. There might be other people in the house when I got home from school, for example, and I might say hi to these people and how interesting and noisy that might be. Instead, our company was the TV running quietly under everything.

* * *

Truly, I was only there with you in the warehouse because that past January I'd gotten hit by a car. It was a beautiful day in Brooklyn, one of those perfect ones with backlit clouds. I had my headphones on and a square leather bag with a thin strap. I was on my way to work and I was being moody. Earlier that morning I'd picked up my roommate's copy of Rebecca Solnit's *Hope in the Dark*, left on the kitchen table, and I'd read just the first line about how "your opponents would love it if you were hopeless." I'd stopped reading because I was late, which of course, I always was. I never know what time it is. I rushed out of my apartment, thinking about hope and how I didn't have any. I was walking and breathing, breathing and thinking and crossing the street like any person does, when I was interrupted. A fissure opened in the day and my breath stayed in my chest. I became a doll in the air, thinking, yes, take my day away, because I hadn't wanted to go to work. As if watching from the sky, I was aware that the softness of my body had been dented by metal and moved up and forward like a laugh. There was no pain at all, just the thud of my body falling back to the ground, then skidding. I was somewhere else.

What does anyone want after they've been hit by a car besides their mom? I called you but you didn't answer so, next, I called someone I'd been sort of seeing. I called her while leaning over the sink, taking a swig of coffee like a cool guy. I'd left the hospital before meeting with a doctor. My lover sent a car, and by the time you called me back, I was in her arms. I crouched up out of her floor futon bed to talk to you. There was classical music from WNYC playing in the background of a very fancy loft space in Williamsburg and a ringing in my head that was starting to spread far out. This was in 2008.

No, I didn't stay in the hospital, I said into the phone. No one was coming to my room and I was hungry.

Well, I'm coming, you said. I'm just coming down.

I held the phone away from my head and looked around to see if something strange was happening out the window, a wind or something bending the trees back, but there was no wind. The joy that shook me was a cage of bingo balls. I felt like grabbing my jacket and running down the street into the rain, but it was sunny. I couldn't think of one time that you'd come to help me. The unevenness of this had always been painful.

All my life, I was the person who held your hair back while you vomited. I'd kneel on the carpet of your bedroom watching you shallow breathe. I was always waiting. I'd watch you disappear into someone else's house, waving back at me like I was not your child. As an adult, I put up boundaries like I thought was a good idea, except mine were never strong, they were loose traffic cones or a paper chain of people holding hands, flimsy things waving red for a bull. Come on, love me, please, is all I was ever saying.

This moment—the car accident—made you run toward me. Immediately, I wanted more accidents. Like I said, I was twenty-two.

* * *

Mom, being your child was being in a haunted house. We'd jerk to the right or left with life and your ponytail would swing from side to side. The lights would be bright in my face and you'd see ghosts and hear whispers and some days we'd be delighted. You'd pull the car over and ask me to roll the body of a crow into a box, pushing its wet body around with a stick. You'd cry and cry until I did it. You'd sneak us into hotel pools on each of my birthdays. You'd get overwhelmed, get drunk, turn up Whitney Houston on the tape player or Missy Elliott and swerve into the median on our way back home.

There were men and cocaine and fast cars and then farm trucks. You sped through everything. I'd carry your train at your weddings. I do think you tried to reciprocate my care for you, but your mind was bent sideways like in some major wind. I hadn't chosen this ride, but neither had you.

For so long a self-imposed pessimism had guided my interactions with you: I was sure I'd be hurt. For years I had tried to force you into the role of my antagonist. I'd been doing this daily at any mention of *mom* since I was seventeen.

As I got older, I started seeing my body grow into yours. Whenever I was actively working to forget you, I'd look down at my own hand and I'd see that the same slight turn of your pointer finger to the left was suddenly mine in exactness. I'd wish for my fingers and neck to thicken so I wouldn't see traces of you there anymore. I'd delete your number. I'd yell into the night at you. I'd rip up your pictures and put the pieces in a drawer. I lived as your shadow in the city, doing things you wouldn't like doing or wouldn't approve of. I was having threesomes, and smoking and chewing gum at the same time, and walking slowly over the bridges at night. I was also going to marches and reading on the train. I was sitting in those vast New York libraries and looking up at the ceilings. I protected myself.

* * *

Reading my roommate's book in the kitchen that morning in 2008, I hadn't yet gotten to Solnit's thesis, the idea that hope "is an embrace of the unknown and unknowable, an alternative to the certainty of both optimists and pessimists."

I'm only now reading this part of the book and it's seventeen years later.

When you got to Brooklyn that evening to rescue me, you'd driven the seven hours straight with no breaks. You hadn't been in New York since we lived there when I was two and you were an au pair on the Upper East Side. I was waiting on the street for you to pull up and I watched you put your hand in front of your eyes to shield them from the lights. You had to pee badly, you said, and we laughed about you doing a pee-pee dance on the sidewalk where I'd been splayed out nine hours before. You smiled to match my smile. We could have been anywhere, but you'd come to care for me and that was better than being at the beach. Do you have any Diet Coke? was your first question. All I had was tap water and Pop-Tarts and chocolate from Trader Joe's, so we ordered jerk chicken from the corner and sat on the floor by the TV with my roommate walking in and out and we connected. We really did. I realized that all along, all those years in New York, I'd been missing you. We didn't always get along, but we belonged together, everyone could see it. That night in my apartment, I decided to let go into this good feeling and lie around with you like on a lounger in a pool. I was too tired to fight off the happiness.

We sat there on the floor and you stared at me. You were transfixed by the blood on my temple and how close to death I'd been. A few inches and it wouldn't have just hit your head at the jaw, it could have taken out your spine versus just flipping you in the air, you'd said. Anything could have happened. You were wide eyed.

Is there something wrong with us, honey? you said.

I looked up at you from poking around at the dirty rice in my Styrofoam container.

We just seem like we can be ourselves together no matter how much time has passed. You'd said "wrong" but you meant things were different for us and great. Your face was so open when you said this.

I heard the soft click of the front door and figured my roommate was leaving somewhere. I hadn't noticed him for hours. We'd been in a little world of our own.

I didn't know what to do with the way you watched me and the way you sat next to me with your hands folded. I felt suspended there. I suddenly feared the burgeoning hope I was feeling. It felt disgusting to me and like a secret.

No, I thought, fuck it, I'll let it happen, and I smiled at you while the streetlight streamed in beautifully.

I couldn't tell anyone what was happening, because they would say nobody ever changes. But what if people do change, what if you do, and what if I miss it?

This is a utopian thought maybe:

There on the floor of my apartment, I imagined a future of us both slowed way down. We'd be smiling and old. I'd get to really connect with you because peace would be everywhere. We would live on the island together. I pictured bringing your groceries into the house for you and maybe making you eggs. I thought you'd have a big floppy dog that I could walk. You could have chickens and a screen door that would slap. From that day on, I lived with this image. I'd make all this happen if you didn't. I'd take care of you.

We stayed in Brooklyn together for a week, looking at each other and watching TV. This was heaven and I didn't get enough of it, so I planned to take a week off work that summer and spend it at your place, just me and you.

* * *

Just yesterday, I had "Dreamlover" loud in my headphones and I was missing you when I looked and saw a fluffed-up bird sitting on the step below a window, dying. Her eyes were closed and her strong nest was just above her on an eave. I hadn't noticed it before. I moved her gently into some shaded moss, and her body puddled into the warm pine needles. The unfinished nest fell off its eave eventually, with no babies in it. She'd been carefully making it all spring, coated the base with mud so it wouldn't shake, some of my hair was visible in the woven moss.

I felt for this bird so strongly. I feel everything so strongly. You gave me this same sensation of being sick with feeling. You passed it on to me but you also brought it up in my body all the time. I'd come to expect it from being together and I spent our life braced for it, which turned into dread. I think this car accident was the one time I'd brought it up for you.

Care is not automatically a burden, and it is not automatically beautiful, writes Leah Lakshmi Piepzna-Samarasinha.

* * *

When I followed you home from the warehouse that summer, you were driving slow for me even though I knew exactly where we were going. We rounded the cheese house, a former wine and cheese store that was literally shaped like a cheese wheel, which had been closed my whole life but everyone called it that still, toward Hinckley's with its beautiful boat hulls formed with untold chemicals, past the yard of the guy who made dragons out of oil cans. You had a ONE DAY AT A TIME bumper sticker with the silver metallic trim and a hand holding a coffee mug. We passed the Trenton lobster pound as the last thing on the mainland. Then the Narrows, that shallow expanse of sea, headed to a fingerprint of land in the greens and clays and blues of low tide.

What's interesting about this place is that it's both fast and slow. Millions of people rush to the island all summer, but in the winter that infrastructure for those millions is empty. That's part of what makes it unique, like night at the museum.

I stayed with Grammy and Grandpa here each summer and winter break from middle school on, and then moved in full-time for the first time when I was nineteen. You were in Dallas that whole time, you'd never lived here until now. When you came to the island two years earlier, you'd dropped your city act really quickly and started wearing flannels and hiking shoes and your shoulders relaxed.

I rolled down my windows to smell the tide, like always, crossing the bay there. It was high, so no big smell, but the water was green in the rocky part and home hit me as exhausting and rich, kelp growing long around the mussel boats out there. What smelled good to me was all the things that die in the sun during an ebb tide. You were the kind of person who'd find a dead crab and talk to it sweetly. You'd made me sensitive but unafraid.

You were staying at Wayne's, Sully's cousin's place, which meant you really did like him, because he didn't have anything to offer you except something from his cousin. You and Sully had been together for a while by then, and it was serious that you were staying together and that you'd invited me. The house was that one-story with split-log siding, a matching garage with green doors. The street was shaded with maples and you were so pumped by how cute it was and how it fulfilled your dream of a woodstove to tend to for focus and a reason to be home, but also a reason to be outside and chop wood and be with your body. This was your woodland self, separate from the Puritan one that you'd been cultivating in response to all the pressure around you to see work as a reflection of personal worth. It's not work if your hands aren't bleeding, you'd say, showing me your hands like I was arresting you. There was always a streak of blood in the crease where your thumbs met your palms. But in the woods you were different—you'd reach into yourself and connect with a steady spirituality, you wanted to be with the woods like friendship. If there is such a thing as a true self, I think this was yours: chopping wood, tending a stove, listening to a breeze in branches.

I pulled in behind you and I noticed I was smiling. I forced my face to neutral because I didn't want to overwhelm either of us with expectations. You pulled in front of me and I heard you jerk your emergency brake.

Sully was there in front of us tooling with his red MG, a 1952 convertible with a hefty British grill and sloping bucket seats. Two squirrels tumbled across the garage roof behind his head. He wiped his hands on his pants. He had gray hair and a short gray beard, wild teeth and red suspenders that matched the car.

Hiya, he said to me, standing up. The wind was behind him, so it was fluffing his beard out. He turned to you. Hi, Katy Q! He put his hand out to sort of catch you. You let him and gave him your hand, but your body was still heading toward the house, so you held each other loosely, looking back at me.

Everything was about to start.

Sully would go do his own thing while I stayed over, down in his camper at the Narrows.

We'll come over and check on you later, you said to him and Sully mumbled always, so I didn't understand him, but I heard him. His flat syllables sounded good through his teeth. There were cars driving by but slowly like summer. The woods around us were quiet and stuffed with fireflies. Honestly, I'd never seen you so in love with anybody. I don't know if you were actually in love but your hair was wavy like you were. I sighed actually. There was nothing to rush about.

When he let go of you, it was slow, and you played like you were running through a field. You bounced up the steps to that front door. The screen door slapped and you called at me from behind it. There was a BB gun with a wooden butt by the back door that you wanted to show me. A bat blew by in front of us, maybe two, because it was early evening. Looking out at the tree line, I could see a little iron triangle in a circle with a small brass bell hanging in the middle of it. Sully was a welder among everything else he was, he'd made it for this purpose.

Watch me, Em, you said, with your boat bag still on your shoulder.

You held open the screen door with your foot and brought the BB gun up, squinting your eye. Another bat flew by. The sound of you hitting the bell went all around the woods. Listen to that echo! you said. Echoes are so cool! You let go of the tight screen door so that it slapped. I followed you with my cheeks warm from smiling. You were excited to show me everything. This was your marksmanship. You'd been learning to change your oil, wearing stained purple Carhartts and a matching duck jacket, climbing from under the car with a grease-slicked mustache to take a selfie for me. You'd been learning to weld too. A photo of you in a welder's helmet, holding a flame, was framed on the cabin's entry table. Dirt-caked muck boots were by the door, a clam hoe was leaning against a bucket. You were happy to tell me about how you'd been putting Fluid Film on it to keep it good even in salt water because now you knew about metal. Sully represented all this learning.

It still smelled like woodstove in there, even though I assumed it hadn't been lit for months. Wayne's place was a small one-bedroom cabin so all the smells skulked around in the heat. You'd made a stack of a sheet, pillow, and quilt folded up on the arm of his couch for me. Wayne's bachelor-leather couch was in stark contrast to the quilt.

Looking around, I saw your hope chest against the back wall, hulking in the corner of the room. You talked about it constantly, this project you'd been working on since I could remember. You were filling it with things for us for after you died. These things had been kept in a big Tupperware for years, until you got an actual wooden chest. I was never tempted to look inside. I don't know why. I sort of associated it with church in the way that churches are always about death. I had the same feeling about the chest as I did that story of the girl with the ribbon around her neck. She teases it her whole life all the way to her deathbed, when finally her husband undoes the bow and her head rolls across the floor.

I've looked up "hope chest" for the first time only recently. I don't know where you'd gotten the idea for one, but the term comes from the practice of mothers preparing trunks for their daughter's eventual marriage, slowly filling it with silverware and heirlooms. All I knew was that my baby teeth and my baby book were in there.

It was your treasure and you were constantly reminding me of where it was. You were building an altar to our time together. Whenever you told me about something you'd put in there, you seemed to be saying, don't forget, I'm going to leave you here at some point. I didn't forget that ever.

Anytime anyone brought up death, you looked wistful. Your relationship to dying was soft fascination with a hint of pleasure, which I get. Though maybe the hope chest was your tether to me, and maybe I was a tether to life.

Remember when those people broke in and I thought your baby book was gone? you'd say once every few months. You were talking about the time we lived off a highway in Dallas, and sometimes people would break in because it was easy to leave quickly from the access road. One of these times, a big window was broken and many things were smashed and there was blood on the carpet. You couldn't find my baby book and you spent all day looking for it on your knees and crying. You'd eventually found it under your mattress, you'd hid it there but forgot, and that's what got you to the store to buy this whitewood chest.

The fact that your hope chest was with you at Wayne's meant you lived here. This was sinking in. I watched you set your boat bag down by the door and go straight to the fridge. The baby frogs everywhere around were starting up, tiny orange-brown peepers with throats that grew into a bubble as a call to mate. The frogs' high-pitched calls had a hue to them. It was dusk. You stood up out of the fridge and flicked on the light above the kitchen sink. It had a garage-style hum to it and we both cringed because you hadn't cooked in there often enough to realize Sully's kitchen lights were blank-white fluorescent. Well, that's awful, you said, looking at me and squinting. It is awful, I said. You flicked the switch off. More white-blue light pooled on the driveway. You stepped into the bedroom and brought a lamp back, set it on the counter by the sink with its checkered red shade, and turned it on. There, you said, making the *T* a *D*. Making your *T*'s into *D*'s was your way of enacting cozy. You didn't talk like that with Sully or anyone else around. Our being together unlocked a safety for you—for both of us. It gave you something you'd needed that wasn't on offer anywhere else in your life, the freedom to be this woodland self who talked in a squeaky-toy voice.

Dere, you said again, I can see you now, and that was funny to us both because it was actually much dimmer.

You getting on in there? Sully shouted from the driveway. He'd heard us laughing about the light. We ignored him. The radio was playing nearly inaudible classical from the kitchen window. It was getting dark.

You must be tired, I said. And as I said it, I realized a headache I'd been nursing had disappeared, which almost never happened. The classical music was covering the hum of the refrigerator, doing its job.

I am always tired, you said, not asking me anything, just making sloppy joes.

I strained to understand because this was the most quiet we'd ever been and the most focused on each other. No TV. It's hard for me to even convey the quiet. It was soft like peeling a banana. You were looking me in the eyes and I felt watered. I didn't know I was a dry plant before your looking. Headlights crossed us both and we stopped to watch someone turning around in the driveway. A breeze started up, the wind chime got going. The last light of the day reached for us and then disappeared.

* * *

Remember how you made Sully stay at the Narrows on my behalf? I guessed you'd asked him to give us space for my visit, which felt kind. I liked that he was there and not there.

I've always loved the Mount Desert Narrows Campground murals of eccentric trees with some purple and green waves on this cistern thing by the front entrance. There were kids everywhere, fires at each little site but only murmured talking for the most part plus laughter from anyone drinking beer.

You had the *Islander* rolled up under your arm as we were walking up to Sully. I was holding your wicker basket filled with marshmallows and napkins and sticks to grill with that you'd packed. We were going to hang out with him for the evening. You put a fleece on over your pink cotton shirt. You were wearing your purple Carhartts with little soft slides. Kids were running by us in the half dark and there was a whole clot of them with Nerf guns aimed toward the sea. Sully's site was closer to the road and I kept thinking, how many guys have I seen you with? Nobody like this. The winter before, when I'd met him, he'd dressed as Santa for your sober group and he held a sprig of holly above your head and kissed you.

My bedtime is at ten, you were saying, walking up to him. His camper's blue awning was out and you wagged your finger. He pulled you toward him by your elbow and you had to stop him from holding on to you by putting your hand on his chest. I'm serious, Mister Dorr, you said. You were laughing. Your hand on his chest was in his hair because he was wearing a Henley T-shirt under his overalls.

The Maine flags on the front office were waving a little and it smelled like fire and propane with some sea.

Was I supposed to comment on your affection? Probably not.

A dog howled. We turned toward it. Motorcycles revved by on Route 1.

Sully lit a little fire for us by the camper and you were talking to him fast, something about Ledgelawn in the paper. You wanted to show him what they said about the Ledgelawn Cemetery because you'd lived in it together in that same little camper while Sully did the metal work on the long cemetery fence. You were talking about many people I didn't know, which was relaxing.

I was sitting in the teal lawn chair furthest from the fire and feeling it through my hands as cool.

A larger group of motorcycles came and went and we all stopped talking because of them. Sully handed me a Coke. Oh, but I brought hot cocoa, you said.

I want to double-fist it all, I said, and you loved it.

You were a painting across from me laughing, Sully's arm around you. We were all laughing about alcoholism. I crossed my legs wide and buried my back into the lowest part of the lawn chair. I'm telling it to you like this because I want you to know how present I was. I cherished this. You were smiling. Sully was unpacking all the lobstering drama and I told you both about the people I was dating in New York and how I thought about taking hormones but decided against it for now and you nodded about it with lips all soft.

You leaned forward to pull s'mores ingredients out of your bag—the chocolate and graham crackers and marshmallows were all already opened but closed with rubber bands. You probably had these since last summer. You both thought it was great that I was eating my marshmallows only after they caught fire and you were waiting for me to do it. You looked at me like you were seeing something new. A strawberry-blond, kind-of-thin dog wandered behind us. Sully reached for it like he'd been reaching for you all day and scratched its haunches. The dog's family called until it left us. Things got even more quiet. I was starting to have trouble hearing you because I wasn't feeling good. The headache had rolled back in. I told you I should probably go to bed and you offered me baby aspirin to chew because I told you I'd already taken Excedrin. I thought the baby aspirin thing was funny because it meant we were both tinkering with NSAIDs. We had the same headaches and bendy joints that hurt and all of it, a constellation of chronic pain that matched up. I liked sharing things with you and I liked that you held the answers to my body in yours to some extent. I can't believe you worked as much as you did with the same pain as me. I really can't grasp it.

Sully stood up and then you did, and he hugged you. Okay, Katy Q, he said with his mustache moving.

A slight fog started up. We almost need heat, you said.

The idea of getting in bed adjacent to each other was nice. I loved all your smells—Clinique? Yankee Candle? You coming up to the couch to pat my leg over the quilt before bed made me want to move in. The quilt on me was pastel pink and yellow. You were saying goodnight with your hand on my knee and a toothbrush hanging out of your mouth—I love you, my honey, you were saying. Maybe you can stay a little longer? You'd made your voice small to say that last part. You rubbed your eyebrow with your sleeve, which felt warm to watch. Grammy told me that you'd had a little sock doll as a kid that you did it with and I loved picturing you still loving your doll like *The Velveteen Rabbit.* Every time you did laundry, I'd find you rubbing your eyebrow with a warm sock. You made me sad often, just like that book.

Wait, let's see if I can do it in the dark, you called from the bathroom. There was the sound of your toothbrush landing in a glass and then you were back in the living room. You picked up your BB gun and pushed the door open, stuck your foot out against the screen door, brought the butt to your shoulder long enough for a breeze to rush in.

The pellet's sound was crisp and I felt something settle around it. I think you were proving a point. You turned to me, grinning, waiting for my reaction. See? you said, and you meant the sound. I smiled back. You were lit up by your own precision. I felt the pull to praise you, but what were you doing playing with guns?

Later, as I was falling asleep, you were in the kitchen, checking something on the stove. I watched you move through the light and your shadow flickered like something glitching. I don't know why it upsets me now to remember this.

* * *

My first full day staying with you at Wayne's, you had to go to your housekeeping job at the inn, so you sent me off to work for

Willie. I imagined that I wasn't invited to go with you to work because that would mean I'd sit in the lobby writing under lamp-light on old couches and drink their complimentary coffee or lemonade and I would be comfortable, which was not something that worked for us. You wanted me to have bleeding hands like you and if I didn't, this was bad somehow because I was your reflection and what you needed reflected back was productivity.

Maybe this wasn't even it. Maybe you didn't want me to watch you clean toilets. I have no idea. All I know is that you never wanted me there, so it was rare I saw this nine-to-five version of you. On this trip, you only wanted me to hang out at the warehouse, otherwise, we'd meet at your place after work. If you'd had a little bit of rest, you were a person smiling and eating something fun, wearing a robe watching *E! News* and scrolling Pinterest on your phone, gossiping with me. I expected this was mostly going to be our time together, but I was hopeful for even the most rare version of you, the one that had a lot of rest—like more than two days of rest–when we'd suddenly be in this new present place with each other. It felt like walking into a cavern or something, my eyes had to adjust. You talked in a completely different voice and were kind of in *Fantasia*, everything seemed to respond to you because you were full of unmatched awe and gratitude, the clouds danced, the leaves shook. You were humble and in reverence, we'd talk in low voices and would hold hands. I wonder often if this way of being was your baseline, which rarely emerged because you always had to work.

That first morning on the visit, you'd left for work long before I got up. I pictured your walk to the housekeeping entrance. You'd pass by the *Margaret Todd*, a four-masted schooner with stains on its white hull and enormous red sails luffing, docked just out front of the hotel, and you'd pretend you were in another century. Sometimes they would move you from the main building to the modern one by the pool and you didn't like that, but you liked your tips and the hours because you were home by one, or two if you had to go to the grocery.

The sea gives and the sea takes, Willie was yelling because a wave was laughing up his glove, bobbing in the foam just beyond this pink seawall in this lady's yard. The tide took one of my gloves, he yelled.

He had to hold up his shorts by the belt as he was coming over the wall, laughing while he was pulling his pants up and hauling around. Here's another bucket, he said and pushed his hair back from his forehead, passing me the orange Home Depot bucket he'd been using for weeds. He'd shown me what a weed was and didn't care if I was wrong a few times between flower and weed in the mulch. He was a great boss this way. This was in Bass Harbor at a little cape on the end of this residential road with nobody home. The pink seawall and the spongy ground underfoot were great. I'm gonna go check on Brad and everybody at Rock Cove, he said. He was about to leave. I'm glad you're keeping an eye on your mom! He was talking with his back toward me, loading a rake and a barrel of leaves into the bed of his truck. He was wearing his teal shirt with that big sun on it, cargo shorts, and green Crocs.

Yeah?

Yeah, he said, turning toward me. She's glad to be with you. She's been talking about it every day for six months. Have fun! He clapped me on the back and hopped into his little red truck with everything in the bed, trash cans and Weedwackers and rakes and shovels, cans of Mountain Dew rolling around. He waved and peeled out of the thin driveway onto Route 102.

The little pink seawall was granite and a line against the harbor. The house had a mini lighthouse as a mailbox and this small lawn with circular mulch beds and a hedge in the back. A couple of heavy Old Town kayaks were pulled up by the seawall. The view was of lobster pots on floats and then ten or so boats on moorings.

My coffee was in a ruined paper cup and I was shaded by a few leafy maples. I could just walk into the sea and sit there. Somebody walked by in Grundens and set Willie's soaking glove on the step and shot up a hand as a wave. The ground was spongy. Seagulls did everything above me. I'd been reading nautical charts of the area on my phone to understand how deep it actually was, probably in the thirties or fifties out there. Only in the water does it feel good to have a body.

A storm would have been nice at the moment, I was thinking, with lightning cracking toward where the eagles were near Bass Harbor Light and a musty rain. I was hot. Each wave was soft instead, a steady navy-blue white mixed with the noise of neon lobster pots and buoys and boats out there. There were overflowing bougainvillea and cosmos in purples and pinks in every window box. You'd always said that I should be working with my hands, and it did feel good for my mind to be out there doing that. This was a puzzle though, because sometimes my body hurt too much to move it for my mind to feel better. I didn't let myself rest either, almost ever. I thought about it. I was tired. The car accident had slowed things down for a few weeks but overall my life was *no sleep, bus, club, another club,* etc.

Being on the island was like when the train goes above ground on the Q and you can suddenly see how fast you're moving. This was hitting me out there, but I wasn't ready to stop. I needed to be in the city, things would be too slow otherwise. I really had internalized much of what you had, that I needed to grit my teeth and push through everything: pain, overwhelm, overstimulation, panic, lack of sleep and money and peace… I had to leave the body to do this and I'd been in that state for so long, I wasn't totally sure how to get back in. I don't think we ever talked about this but we should have.

I was judging by the '50s little pillows with tulips on them and the metal furniture on this house's back porch that this was a house belonging to one of Willie's ladies who he loved. He was going after work for pedicures with eighty-year-old Grace and invited me. I hoped for another real good day with you, so I said no. Driving back, I wanted to get you something as a thank you. I figured I could buy you some fancy birdseed and a birdhouse from Salsbury's, burn all the money I made. I just wanted to give you all my money anyway. I took a last dirty swig of coffee with two Excedrin and the sunlight moved across the water in a perfect way. Each wave was calling up high tide.

I rested on my knees in the mulch. My knees were wet through my pants because of the soil. I just let it happen for a minute before snagging a raspberry out of the thicket by the rosehips and heading to my car. I texted Willie that I was heading out. He sent me a thumbs-up immediately. I put WERU on the radio, which was playing New Potatoes or something Celtic. My drive was what I wanted, quiet and sunny with puffy low clouds moving across the sun at a clip. Two bald eagles circled above the lake on my way back. I stopped on the shoulder to look and then pulled forward and parked the wrong way at the guardrail place to swim. Nobody else was there, which got me out of the car. Soft waves were moving in the direction of Beech Mountain and the banks of the little beach on that lake with its small swimming square made with ropes and buoys for kids. I pulled my shirt over my head and was left with my regular shorts. I laid my shirt and my towel on the rock and pushed myself into a shallow dive on the top layers of cold lake. My head broke into the water and my whole body came up happy. My head was light, my arms were weightless and my legs too. I frogged around for a while. There were long grasses there and some fish. I swirled my feet to keep from touching the fish. I worried about making it to Wayne's before you, so I only stayed in the water for a minute or two and then stood right up where I'd been swimming and trawled back to the bank. The rock was warm for me to lean on and dry off my legs. There were cars going by but nobody stopping. I got back in the car dripping but wrapped in a towel.

Salsbury's was just past Wayne's, and I wondered if it would be strange to go in still damp, but it was summer. The cedar-sided building smelled like potting soil, aisles lined with clay flowerpots and racks of seed packets. I grabbed the bag of birdseed with the cardinals on it, which seemed fancy. I also found a cedar birdhouse with a copper roof, the nicest one in there.

Driving back uphill toward Wayne's, I worried that Sully would be there when I pulled in, but he wasn't. Nobody was. I set the things out for you by the woodstove. My phone was on one percent. I looked at it. It was 2:01. I sat on the edge of the couch to wait and watched for you out the window like a dog.

* * *

You'd filled a boat bag with tuna sandwiches and chips and the seltzers that I liked on my last morning. I was wearing this striped shirt and blue cotton shorts and was letting you drive us, which wasn't typical. You had your little film camera on the top of the boat bag because we were making a memory. Grammy loves the story of when you were in a snowstorm one year during your visit and you were trying to scrapbook together. She would put one square of colored paper behind her pictures, and by the time she looked up, you'd have drawn detailed lace frames and made small paper flowers to put inside of little paper pockets you'd made. She thought this was the funniest thing in the world and would laugh and laugh telling us about how bad hers was in comparison. I wished she was with us that morning because you and I were having the best time. I figured maybe now that you and I were making these inroads, we could be all three of us again soon. I'd tell Grammy it was great and you knew that. Maybe the camera was to show her.

The drive to the trailhead wound past Northeast Harbor on the right. The boats all clustered there against small pine-dotted islands and gleaming water: dinghies, white ugly angular yachts with Australian flags, pretty Morris sailboats, and perfect Hinckley picnic boats in the arm of this thin harbor, pines on either side. Money was just floating there in front of this sheer cliff on our left. Around the bend was a pond, framed by mountains with that dog-friendly waterbody to the sea, old boathouses, marsh. Between the two were those sheep and horses in the wooden fence on the hillside. We were hiking Thuya. There was a tiny parking lot across from the cliff and a carved wooden door. You pulled into it and yanked the brake.

I'd never been anywhere more beautiful, is the truth. Juniper and pitch pines hugged these mossy cliffs with waving rosemary and lavender lining deer paths. At Wayne's, I'd given you that birdseed and a birdhouse as an offering for bringing me around all of this. You were happy about the birdseed. I think the birdhouse too.

Oh, I'll put it up when I have my own place sometime, you'd said. I hadn't seen Sully since the Narrows, so I wondered if things were okay.

There was a long gravel path with thistle and huckleberry in handfuls along the graded incline. You walked us to a red-roofed shelter with branches holding it together and a cedar bench. It was on the side of this cliff overlooking the harbor. You were making me a map. You smelled like vanilla walking by me and into the shelter. I love the forest, you said, but I know you love the sea, so here we are. I can show you so much more like this, you were saying, looking out at the treetops. You'll have to come back.

We sat down with the boat bag between us. It was early afternoon, a lobster boat was motoring into the harbor. You were in your Sketchers and those purple Carhartts, and I realized this was your one day off. Maple leaves mixed with balsam and rustled behind us. I watched the manicured pines stay still. I love these trees, I said, looking off to our left at the clump of them twisting with flat needles off the cliff. I think they're my favorite.

Ocean trees, you said, so that makes sense. You handed me the tuna sandwich you'd made. Thank you so much for bringing me here, Mom. It's amazing. The color of the water was unreal against the trees. Your glasses reflected it.

Let's take a pic, you said, shaking out your Olympus from the boat bag and then from its little black case with purple piping. A mini white butterfly moved by.

I held my soda by the neck and leaned toward the cliff into the sun and cheesed for you. My cheeks went high up to my eyes, and I smiled with my teeth, which I never did, because of my snaggletooth. But I'm all yours, I thought, so I let it fly for your scrapbook or whatever this was for.

A few raindrops dashed across the shelter roof seemingly from nowhere. Light was everywhere except just over us, a purple-blue cloud lowered. We looked at each other with mouths open like we were surprised and in a '90s movie. Fresh rain clouded us in for just a few minutes, making it so we were part of it—this is for us, you whispered in that moment of the crash of rain, the island wants you here.

* * *

This want of yours for me to move back was part of a constellation of hopes you talked about on loop all the time, like wanting to make your dad proud and having a veggie garden someday. You had hope everywhere. Your screennames and emails were always love2hope since AOL, you had complicated cookie cutters with *hope* in a scrawl, pillows with angels on them under a *hope* banner and the reverse: angels holding pillows with a tiny embroidered *hope*. You listened to gospel about it and you'd gotten stationary with *hope* as a whole border that you'd written me notes on for decades. Anytime someone suggested being hopeful about something, I'd cringe, and then feel an angry hurt just after that: nothing you'd wanted ever materialized.

Recently, I saw this scene from *Girls* over my wife's shoulder. She was watching it in the kitchen. Hannah's mom talks to her about losing her own mother:

"You think that you've accepted that your mother wasn't that good, and then you realize that you've always had this hope that there would be a conversation where the two of you would have some kind of breakthrough."

They're sitting at a table outside a hospital. Char stopped it and played it back for me. You say this all the time, she said.

"When they die, that conversation can never come," the mom continues.

I nodded because I do talk about that particular grief a lot, about all my wants that died with you. I wanted no conflict, no drugs, no men, live chickens, bad weather, picnics, dinners, reality TV, holidays that weren't sorrowful, birds blowing around and no dead ones, no mice in the house, no floods, no car problems, no courts or jails or hospitals or morgues.

Honestly, I would have liked more memories of us having city days in Ellsworth or Bangor, anywhere that meant an hour drive, so we could listen to train sounds on tape like we'd do to pretend life was slow. I would have liked more memories of us exploring Schoodic and looking out at that lighthouse in the middle of those bays. We could have waded around trying to see all the starfish by the reversing falls or we could have made flower crowns in some fields by the bridge. We'd done this in Dallas somewhere once, the soft eraser of petals between our fingers. A she-loves-me, she-loves-me-not kind of thing, our feet brushing in the grass.

Instead, I have way too many memories of only one of us being able to get comfortable at a time. This felt like holding the corners of a blanket too small to cover us both like in the thick of sleep, an irritated or cold sleep, when there's not enough and pulling, apologizing. My being around depleted your resources from the start.

Mom, I wanted to pay you back. I wanted to make it so we had anything we ever wanted. I was so close to doing it, but just as soon as I thought I could, you let go.

* * *

There was a whole thing that I never wanted to talk to you about directly. I was always vague about it because I didn't want to say anything that could hurt you or make you jealous, but years after this visit, in 2016, I'd bought land on the island with a few friends. It was a long piece that was wet and had been clear-cut at least twice and no one else seemed to want it, but it abutted a cove. Our plan was to live there when we were old and had no more use for the city, but in the meantime I could build you a place on it and you could quit working and have chickens like you wanted.

I was worried all this would make you feel bad, you hated your subsidized development and you'd always wanted to live somewhere else, somewhere deeper into the woods and quiet.

When it had gone on the market, my friend from the grocery I used to work at called me and said I should go look at it, so when I was on the East Coast for work, I made an appointment with a realtor. I didn't tell you anything about this at all and I left without seeing you, back to LA.

When I walked the land for the first time on that trip, I followed a sloping trail from meadow to marsh to mossy hillside through pines that opened onto a rock outcropping in a cove. I cried because it smelled just like Thuya and the Hunters Brook

Trail. The feeling of living like we had when we spent that week together was overwhelming. My ego could die off and I could walk to the sea. I could put all the clocks and calendars away. I could learn the trees and my feet would walk on this sponge ground and I could take even one deep breath. I pictured myself in a little wooden sailboat with a square sail, wearing suspenders and being short and old and happy.

Years and years passed since our visit together and for that whole time, whatever city desk I sat at, in New York and then LA, I would watch *Deadliest Catch* on loop and think about Sully and his son on their fishing boat. I'd picture you out there surrounded by bait stink with a picnic basket, wearing a dress with tiny sleeves and flowers shaped like cherries, looking like your mom looked when she was your age, like Sophia Loren in *Houseboat* with your hair wavy still.

Wherever I was, I fought the pull. I thought about you more than I should have. I was embarrassed about my desire for us all to be together.

The older I got, though, the more my system was seeming to fray. I know I was supposed to live in a city and wear a leather harness at parties and be around more people like me, but I was getting so tired and sick. I was opening my car door after driving home from work to vomit from pain. The city lights had become one streak of bright discomfort. I was feeling like I'd started fumbling my lines everywhere, at coffee shops when I ordered or when I was doing my laundry at the laundromat. I'd try to say hi, how's it going, but it would come out as a mumble and I'd think how I'd rather be under a blanket with Nintendo and playing with slime I ordered off the internet, or reading boat books and watching videos about the sea.

By the time I was living in LA, I was lighting a pine-scented candle before bed each night and looking east. I was squinting all the time and uncomfortable. I took a weekend sailing class because I thought maybe it was the water I was missing. In the bay out by the airport in Marina del Rey, we motored in our rental boat by the docks, flanked by a quiet throng of mako sharks. The belly of airplanes trucked over us one after the other. All light was eaten in their shadow, powerboat motors rang out.

I thought about how at my Dallas middle school, for that eighth-grade superlative thing, I was voted most likely to be a shipbuilder in Maine. I'd done a presentation in class about ships and boat parts and that's what made everyone think so, but I really wanted to be cooler than that. That was the same year I came back from visiting Grammy and Grandpa on the island and you'd turned my room into a boat. You'd gotten me a hammock like I wanted instead of a bed and you put a big ship's wheel on a pedestal and a sail flag across the ceiling and this must have been expensive. I did that twelve-year-old thing, where I'd returned from summer break as a self-conscious thirteen-year-old and told you that this wasn't what I wanted at all, I wanted a clear phone and see-through blow-up furniture. I'd crushed you when I wasn't grateful. I lay awake all night in my hammock bed imagining each small sound was you in your room crying about it.

Living in LA was very much a choice, like the desire to have a clear phone in 2002. I didn't want to be somebody who needed to live in a cold, remote place by the sea. I wanted to shake a particular truth: I belonged to you guys and that meant I was like you. Who did I call on that clear phone? Just Grammy.

Right now, the light is dim outside in an afternoon rainstorm we're having. I think about those nights at Wayne's often, maybe because I took photos of them on a film camera and have them hanging around—the sharp BB gun sound is still in my head along with the way your voice lifted.

We're all sensitive around your birthday, which is this week. The vernal pool next to the house is filling up in the rain. You talked about *vernal* all the time, you loved the vernal spring on the quietside.

Earlier today, I stood on the driveway and let the cracks in my boots bubble, water filling around my feet. I let it take up all my time. I find your birthday is much harder than the anniversary of your dying. I bent down to watch the water flood my shoes like a toddler.

Mom, I fought it for years. I waited until I couldn't take it anymore, and then I came home.

* * *

This was March of 2020. I landed in Boston, on my way to you. I'd always wanted to be able to take a big break and come home for a bit. But it was too expensive to rent a place for even a few days, the longest I'd been back for was five nights or so. But when COVID hit, with my job going remote, I realized I could live up on the island while still making the money I was making in LA, at least for a little while.

So I literally packed up all my stuff and got on a plane to be near you. I left my leather jacket in my closet for my roommate and said goodbye. You worried I was going to show up with California plates and I said, Mom, I'm flying. You thought I was going to get turned away at the state border or get killed because I was coming from away. You said be safe over and over. I kept saying, no, no, I'm fine. But LAX did have trash blowing down the shiny tiles by that salad place from an eerie indoor wind, and I'd never seen anything as empty as the gate for my midnight flight from Tampa Bay to Boston, where I drank a very cold Coke from a vending machine and could hear the echoes of footsteps. Returning to the rows of empty seats from the vending machine, I found a pile of books on the ground. It looked like someone had just dropped the books and run. At the bottom of the pile, upside down and splayed open toward the end, was Virginia Woolf, *To the Lighthouse*: "Now after a little flagging and hesitation the sails filled and, shrouded in profound silence, she watched the boat take its way with deliberation past the other boats out to sea."

* * *

I borrowed my friend's truck in Portland and drove with a thunderstorm Downeast and over the bridge toward Moneskatik. I had driven this route for twenty years but this was the strongest I'd ever felt the wind. It was moving his Tacoma from side to side and I felt like I was riding. It could be the last scene in *Rebecca* when they're hurrying to their house. I was almost scared.

Along the route, I stayed for a bit at my buddy's farm in Greene where they had baby chickens that just hatched. I befriended one brand-new chick who had stargazing syndrome, which we knew because her little neck was bent toward the sky. I guess it was a hereditary vitamin-B deficiency, which I've also got. It's part of the larger group of pains and symptoms we share—you and me, and Grammy too—Ehlers-Danlos syndrome, though I find that diagnosis more helpful than either of you did.

The chick's neck was shaped with her head touching her back so that it prevented her from eating or drinking, like she was always looking at the stars. Her warm roost with her family was a hundred feet from where I was staying. For the first few days,

I watched her miss out on eating when it was harder for her and everyone else was hungry. Eventually, when I couldn't stand it any longer, I reached down and scooped her up. I supported her tiny head with my fingers and we went to breakfast together or to the pond or to sit softly on my bed in this tent. I was staying in a wall tent with a little Buddy Heater in it that she and I would sit in front of. Her feathers would fluff when I'd bring out the dropper to feed her and spill tiny beads of water into her open mouth. The wind tussled the spruce near my tent. I liked her heartbeat beneath my fingers.

I was feeling pretty good out there, and teaching on Zoom was pretty nice. Stargazer would sit on my chest, and I would lay down. Kids would yell and whoop in the fields and the roosters would crow and Stargazer and I would cuddle our loose bodies together and I was sorry she wasn't with her family. It occurred to me that I'm one of three generations bent the same way from EDS, how nice is that? I've never really been alone.

The morning I left the farm, I walked up to the chicken gate and instead of running up to me, as she'd been doing, Stargazer stayed back. I watched as her little family encircled her and they ran back to their roost as one. She's better, one of the farmers said, which is great. I headed toward the car.

The trees were bent east as I left. Wind chimes started up all around. I looked at the clouds and pulled my shirt closer. Hairs went up on my neck. One far-off thunderclap traced a finger across the sky in lightning and it cracked near my head. I was about to move into a wharf room that had been an Airbnb but was closed in COVID. I'd rented it from a nice lady over Facebook. The house was near you, with waves booming all around and salt crystals caking the windows. I'd lean against those windows and I'd sit on some other person's couch.

Walking toward my car, my stomach was suddenly heavy. This was the feeling of being sick. I wasn't sure what I was sick with. I was nauseous, which maybe meant I was very excited. The sky went a fairy-tale purple.

* * *

Honestly, Mom, I've been on a beach looking at a perfect sunset with Creamsicle colors and an enormous moon rising over teal water with a lover or a friend, for example, and I've been ill at ease. I've itched about the waistband of my jeans or the heat of the sand or something like that, unsurvivable under my feet. I've thought all I want to do is get back to my notebook that would be sitting on a bedside table in a warm ocean town. Not that I don't love a beach—

Oh no, it's going to be a nice string of weather, Grammy would say to you and me. It's horrible, all this sun, you'd answer, blinking behind your glasses. When are we going to get a break? I'd sit with my legs crossed at the ankles and a notebook, chewing on a yellow pencil and would nod at you both. You'd make a wreath around me like hanging around a horse's neck, I was a winner.

What did you put in this chowder, Mom?

Tomato sauce.

Did I see the mobile groomer over here the other day?

Yes, we thought we'd try her.

How'd it go?

You tell me how it went, Grammy would say, gesturing over to her little white dog with a shaggy, wet-looking face.

We would all laugh. Your voice would go up really high. Grammy knew this was funny and would keep at it until we were all bent over.

Then, when Grandpa would go up to bed and we were really alone, Grammy would lower her voice and say, how's the headaches? This was our meeting. We would look at each other. Not great, we'd all say. Have you tried the headache hat? you would ask Grammy. From CVS? Or I think from QVC but at

CVS? You'd have it with you because you were ready for this meeting. I'll show you. You'd pull a black headband with an ice pack sewed into it from your purse. How's your toe, Mom? Awful, Grammy would say, I can't get a shoe on. We'd start laughing more because she'd show us how she'd cut holes in her sneakers for her toe. I just take scissors to them at this point, she'd say, lifting her foot up to show us. We'd be cackling now.

If Grammy ever had to go into the doctor for any reason, we'd all worry. She'd get admitted for strange, benign symptoms that would land her in there for days. For Grammy, who never wanted to leave the house, this was a nightmare.

You would lean over to me and say poor Grammy.

Grammy would lean over to me and say poor Mom, because you thought you shouldn't eat at all and had to scrub until you bled or run many miles a day to make up for being in pain.

Poor Em, you'd both say, when constantly putting my head down on my desk got me yelled at during school.

The three of us cared for each other in a triangle like carrying grocery bags upstairs.

This is one of my central memories:

You'd pulled into the driveway and I could see your lights click off in advance of your approach. Your keys were making noise. You made it up to the top step carrying your very 1994 backpack purse and you were holding a folder with my name on it. Your eyes were low.

I actually saw a picture of you recently that could have been taken this very same day. You were in that waitressing outfit from when you were working at the Seaman's Inn. In the photo, you are holding a serving tray and wearing a deep-red lipstick and eyeshadow even. Who took it? It was the reenactment village restaurant at Mystic Seaport, so you were dressed in this very particular period black dress with an apron and a doily in your hair. You were wearing this when you came home from my fourth-grade parent-teacher conferences.

You didn't look at me but at Grammy to say in an exasperated way, they said there is something wrong with her.

Maybe it was because you were tired, but a tear fell down your face. It was a marvel and took your makeup with it. You wiped your eye with your arm. You had many other shades of crying, but not often ones that included tears. You pulled your own arms in and Grammy handed the bowl of something to me and went to hug you.

Still not talking to me, you held on to the railing and started to laugh a little behind your crying. Her teacher told me that she'd never amount to anything, that I should start planning for her to work at McDonald's as the best-case scenario. You wiped away tears with her arm and started to laugh like you were exasperated.

Not even the Seaman's Inn? Grammy asked, her eyes smiling. Your eyes started smiling in response to hers.

Nope, you said, and now you were both looking at me and you put your hand up to talk through the side of your mouth.

The teacher said she was retarded.

Well then, we all are, Grammy said, and moved me with just her hand off where I'd been sitting on the stairs.

I went off and ate my dinner after this, unbothered because in New London, in this giant stone house by the sea, we were great. I could see all our skills so clearly: you could make anything you wanted with thread and paper and needles and yarn. You'd been on TV because of it even, on the *The Home Show* in California. Grammy could remember every movie from 1937 to 1964 and every person in them and who did the costuming and the tune of each soundtrack song, also every scene where there was a continuity error. These talents shook the house. I watched you both like you were gods. Grammy said what was happening to me was words. It could have been anything. It definitely wasn't spelling, I failed all my weekly spelling tests and you tried and tried to help. Grammy decided it didn't matter and hung up all the poems I wrote at eight years old with six-year-old spelling and would throw away my report card before you would find it. If the world didn't see these as gifts, fuck the world, was her thought. Fuck the whole wide world.

* * *

That summer of 2020, when I got to the wharf house I'd rented, the storm was playing across the gray cedar shingles. There were four stairs leading up to a glass slider. When I walked up and pulled the door open, the wind pushed the screen slider away from me and ran around inside, rattled through the windows, went up and down the pipes, through the pillowcases, into the neck of my shirt and through the sleeves. The house seemed to jerk back and forth with the force of water. Wind and water were the same. I let the wind have the door for a minute, left the slider open, and walked in.

Here's the other part of living near you guys that I'd become ready for: I was excited to be disabled together.

I walked into the bedroom and lay down on the bed with my bags around me.

I put one hand on my chest and one hand on my stomach and I inhaled. The enormous pull to be here was finally slack.

* * *

The other day, Grammy put her hands to her face at her wooden kitchen table and started crying into them. I was surprised by her shoulders shaking and I put my hand on her back. I couldn't teach you anything, she said. I think about other grandmothers who taught their grandchildren things and I had nothing to give you. All I've ever done is cook and clean and roll around in this wheelchair. She actually hit it with her palm. She'd been ambulatory most of my life, but in the last ten years or so, she only uses her chair.

Grammy, you taught me everything, I said. You taught me unconditional love. She scooted back and studied my face. I don't know, she said. I really don't know.

I'm sure she's comparing herself to the men in our family. They talk about each other as geniuses a lot. It seems to have something to do with football or lawyering or the military, sometimes it's just about the tone of their voice and how they stand. Men like each other more than I thought. I notice it now all the time. They really think each other is smart. Some of these men talk about you like you wasted your talent and this is a subject that gets me more angry than is possible to explain.

I want to say that there's nothing either of you didn't give me. Very materially, I held your gait so close that it became mine.

The magic of having a body meant that I carried copies of you and Grammy around with me. I'm not a scientist, but I've seen a pattern once in a swarm of bees that looked like a face and I think I was born to both of you like that.

I don't know how to talk about our shared disability, because we have no before. I know right now that I prefer soft trails for walking and not concrete. Here, the land is spongy, so I like to walk the whole thing. I don't like to walk to the park as much because the cement is more aggressive. I like the look of the wheelchair I've used for three years or so, with its thick tires and opalescent frame.

I'd reacted to this year with the mean teacher, followed by many more years of special-ed testing and accommodations, by pushing myself to be as able as possible. It didn't work at all. There was no moment when I crossed a threshold into disability, but there was a point during my last few years in LA where I stopped trying to appear less tired.

In my twenties, I brought a pamphlet about Ehlers-Danlos syndrome to you just after I'd been diagnosed with it. When I was diagnosed, I felt this flutter of acknowledgment and possibility and had gone back to you with it because your symptoms matched—Grammy's did, too, but she'd been diagnosed with childhood arthritis, because as she always said, she dragged her leg to kindergarten, and that worked for her. When I told you,

you asked where the name Ehlers-Danlos came from and I said it's two guys' last names and then you said, then why do we care?

I appreciated your point.

I cared because it helped me get a placard for my car and unlocked accommodation to some extent. I'd been diagnosed all about it, but you didn't want that, which I understood. You associated disability with job loss. Any pain for you was supposed to be private and if it couldn't be, you'd choose to crawl under the house like a dog.

When I rolled up to Grammy in this wheelchair for the first time, we sat with our feet touching and our elbows on our armrests and our heads in our hands and we laughed for hours like always, mostly making jokes about how we both need the wider chair because we have the same butt and then I got up out of it to help her make dinner.

* * *

When I woke up that first morning, it was to the sound of slow buoy clanging and I had every choice of my time available to me. Bobo, my little scruffy dog, was curled up in a square of sun on a rug. I leaned out the kitchen window overlooking the boat launch and hung my elbows out. The morning was a mixture of sun and salt and seaweed and motor- and cooking-oil smells for being across from a restaurant. Little flowers in their boxes on the neighbor's wharf cottage waved, I leaned farther out to see a wooden sailboat, its luffing cream-colored sails.

It was Saturday. I wiped my eyes as the restaurant started up its soundtrack of Coldplay songs. People would sit under the red checkered umbrellas at picnic tables for the rest of the summer listening to "The Scientist." The oven clock said eleven. I hadn't slept that late maybe ever.

I wasn't sure what to do with my adult choices. There were so many. I put on my Crocs and followed the dock out of the apartment. I leaned over the little spot for slips. I'd been to this dock often as a kid to eat fish sandwiches at the restaurant with Grammy and Grandpa, but I'd never noticed the bathroom for the fishermen there by the bait buckets and traps and dumpsters. It had little frosted windows and one toilet that was attached to the building I'd just moved into. It seemed cool and nice that there was a public bathroom in a private house. It occurred to me that I'm nostalgic for times that probably never existed. Sailboats were skating between each other in the harbor, tenders pointed out each mooring, a couple of lobster boats were tied up and unloading, a big yacht pulled in behind the *Alice B*, Willie's sailboat *Eden* was out there too with her white bowsprit pointing into the wake from a lobster boat heading out.

The apartment was at the front of a long building that jutted directly into the sea. There was no one else in the building. I was all alone with thick oak trim and vinyl floor. It had a giant TV and the lady didn't make me sign anything to move in. I was surrounded by WILD AND FREE JUST LIKE THE SEA and I LOVE YOU TO THE BEACH AND BACK nautical Hobby Lobby wall art. I watched from the dock as a refrigerator truck boomed by within inches of the building through a tiny alley. This caught my breath. They'd do that all day to pick up lobsters. The sun was so warm and seaweed lazed around the top of the water: I called you.

Hearing your voicemail where you said your own number was doubling. My thoughts started churning. You knew I was getting in last night. I clicked on your number and double called you sort of impulsively. Where were you? My face made the kind of blank frown that felt heavy to do.

You didn't call me back for several days. We were about to begin this dance. It was the same one I'd watched you and Grammy do for years. We would struggle to find each other across this island of bare mountains. You were twenty minutes down the road.

When you called me back it was several nights later and we were having another storm. Lightning cracked above the coast guard station. I found out the next day that one of those lightning strikes had lit a fire across the water.

Honey, I'm feeling scared, you said.

Oh. Are you okay? Do you want me to come over? I could wear a mask and come inside?

This storm is big, you responded, not directly answering me. I paused.

I'd pulled a chair up against the kitchen window to look at the water and talk to you. I leaned forward to hear better, I couldn't tell if you were crying.

Do you know I drove to work tonight at 6 p.m. thinking it was 6 a.m.?

I took a beat.

I definitely should have come prepared to be near you in whatever state you were in, but I was caught up in the dream. Here's the truth: I had told everyone that I was only here for a short time, but really, I was hoping I'd get to stay. I tucked this truth under lots of things. My friend Jamila, another collaborator on the land, had been encouraging me to refinance the mortgage into a construction loan. Look, they'd said, you could earn equity if you built on it and plus you could live there and cut out all your rent costs. It's okay to do something like this for yourself, they'd said. Could I still live here if you were drinking, though?

You said it again: do you know I drove to work tonight at 6 p.m. and I thought it was six in the morning? Honey, something's wrong with me, you said. Your *was* slurred. Your *honey* was clear though.

* * *

I'd catch the song you'd sing for us as kids in my head while I was doing dishes in the wharf house:

Oh boy! I've got joy. I do, do you? / It starts in my heart, and spreads to my head.

This was all I could remember, so I went and looked it up. It came with a dance:

> Oh boy! I've got joy. I do, do you? (clap hands and sway hips) /
> It starts in my heart, and spreads to my head /
> And the best place it shows is below my nose /
> I've got joy! (hug self) /
> (whisper, with hands cupped around mouth like telling a secret) Oh boy!

You were always equally full of joy and sorrow. The things you did to cope with this undercurrent of loneliness, you hid. I understood this, I was afraid of anyone knowing the things I did to cope too: knowing about being cozy, about singing "Oh

Boy, I've Got Joy" in a high-pitched voice. What was sucking was that I didn't expect that you wouldn't want to connect. You stopped returning my calls entirely a few weeks after I arrived and I had to sink into the reality that I was alone in my place and you were alone in yours. Months went by with just texts between us. I was ten miles down the road and we didn't see each other once. All of this, my being here, was an experiment in being your neighbor.

* * *

Here's the thing, Mom, I spent my childhood cautioning you like a little bird with a chorus: live, I'd say with whatever force. You kind of always seemed to be teetering there, like I'm saying. If I'm honest, you never seemed to want to. I tacked you down like a sail and we blew around. Of course, all this effort I put into you living meant I was well aware of you dying. I'd forecasted the disaster but not its form. All the same, I've learned that anticipation is not protection.

Right now, I wish we could watch the *Deadliest Catch* season together with the whole recap of the scallop boat disaster on the *Saint Patrick*. I think it was season 2 or 3. I watched all the seasons this winter and I've been thinking of this a lot: the *Saint Patrick* was fishing in the Bering Sea when the crew was caught in a storm and a huge wave hit the wheelhouse, breaking several windows. The captain said, this is it everybody, and so the crew got on their survival suits and jumped into the sea. By the time a rescue team arrived, there were only two survivors washed up on outer islands. Both thought they had survived sinking, but when the coast guard helicopter flew them over their abandoned boat, it was upright and floating. They didn't need to jump into the frigid water that killed them at all. The boat was completely fine.

That was the worst part, the two men who survived said in interviews. The disaster they were running from only came because they were running.

The only way that I've been able to make sense out of this thing, one of the survivors, Wally Thomas, said, is that I was supposed to be the witness. If somebody needed to know something about this, it was my job to let them know.

I've been rewatching *Deadliest Catch* from this house by a working waterfront, surrounded by people who fish and talk of fishing. All my immediate neighbors are lobstermen, their trap shacks clanging all day, mini cranes and excavators stacking metal, laughter and *fuck you*s mix with the smell of bait and drift through the windows all summer.

I sit in the bathroom with the door open and hear laughter echoing all around the woods. I sink into the tub. My shoulders drop from my ears for one second before they shoot back up because

I'm bathed in guilt. Shock is still leaving my body. I was here when the sheriff came to tell me. We sat right where I am sitting now—the mashed-together beginning and end.

I walk your invisible paths: the doctor I went to last week is the one you recommended I try at one point. I went by accident on a referral. He was standing over me, excited to do a procedure and he beamed a light into my face. At that moment, I realized I should say, do you remember my mom? But then I'd have to say, she killed herself, and I'd watch his face slip between shock and pain, not shock that she would, necessarily, but shock that I'd talk to him about it when he was busy.

Mom, I go absolutely everywhere with you. I'm jolted by every single blue 2006-era Corolla because my emotions crash from excitement that it might be you, to knowing you're dead, to being worried I caused it, to forcing myself out of fault. I'm left here with the project of living.

* * *

Yesterday a big barred owl flew from the eastern pine right onto my porch railing and it looked like a person sitting there. The owl was here to hunt the squirrels that I was incidentally feeding from your feeder. I would have sent you the video I took of the owl. I feel like I am here waiting but I don't know what for. I want you to write something to me in the fogged-up mirror after my shower or to take a glass of water out of my hand and spill it across a table. These are nightmares and my dreams.

I have been sitting here thinking of that boat that didn't sink. Thomas said the crew tied themselves together in the water after jumping. Their life raft had floated away. All night, his job was unclipping his dead crewmates from their life jackets so the living ones wouldn't get dragged under.

Eventually it was just him and one other crew member. She survived the night with him, but he could see her getting tired. He coached her for hours, not knowing where his strength came from.

Then a helicopter flew over them, didn't see them, and left.

He said the light went out of her eyes almost as soon as the helicopter crossed the horizon.

She died clipped to him. He unhooked her, there in the waves, and watched her body drift into layered dark.

He screwed his face up in the interview, this is awful, he said. You don't know what it's like until it's happening.

In our story, I'm hesitating to unclip you.

Originally, you wanted to name me after the story of a kid lighthouse keeper from the *Keep the Lighthouse Burning, Abbie* book, which you'd read with me a lot. In it there's a bad storm on Matinicus and this seventeen-year-old has to keep the lights lit for her father, who is lost at sea.

"I was afraid for you," the dad says in the book when he finally makes it back. "Every night I watched for the lights, every night I saw them," he says, "then I knew you were all right."

You loved this book.

I keep thinking you'll show up like that dad, just when I'm too tired of everything.

"I kept the lights burning, Papa," says Abbie at the end and there's a soft illustration of them hugging, her braids float down her back and mix with his flannel shirt.

I've never slacked on my job of looking out for you. This muscle is still so strong. I try to relax, but it flexes.

Right now, a rainstorm is melting the ice on the roof and dripping down my chimney pipe and onto my bookshelf. There's a soft drip going into a bucket on a stack of books, matching the sap dripping into the buckets outside.

Someone recently said to me, maybe it's better that your mom isn't here anymore. Maybe she saved you many years of more of the same.

I wonder if you can feel people thinking this. I don't think it. I told the person that I longed for something to go well for you, that this longing is still there and is sharper.

* * *

That first summer on the island, I'd drive past your house, looking for the light of your year-round Christmas tree in the kitchen. During lockdown, a heat-sensing camera would have seen only me in my house on the whole block. At night, only emergency-type hallway lights looked on in the coast guard barracks. The bell buoys chimed and the lapping of tide drummed on the launch. Something was actually coming over me out there. I'd bring the trash out back and think, if I fell in nobody would know for a long time. The buoys were half-submerged bodies, face down and tied up to depth. I had nothing to say. Quiet was making its way through everything.

I'd buy the five-dollar sea lavender the lady on my block was selling and stick it in my top buttonhole. I'd offer to bring you some but you'd text back saying, no, honey, not now, maybe when my season ends. I'd watch the thin sidewalk maple scratch and scratch the corner of the slider, particularly in the rain.

By this point, you were working at Salt Cove. A year-round private estate job that you'd gotten because a boss of yours from the inn moved over there and wanted you to go with him. Your detail cleans were perfect and the very wealthy family was obsessed with you. You sent me pictures of thousands of purple butterflies you'd cut and arranged over table-length birch branches, candles that flickered inside ice you'd frozen into molds as luminaria. For their wedding, they'd requested a life-size stupa and you'd worked through the night to gold-leaf an enormous amount of foam board.

You wore an earpiece by the pool so they could call you for an outfit change. You dog-sat for their golden doodles, learned to hand-wash Dior, got COVID at least three times because you'd said they didn't like masking. The man you worked for ordered specialty loafers embroidered with virus balls as a joke during peak pandemic. You had to upload them into their iPad database for clothes so they could see their Maine closet from Milan. I hated their terrible teal family color that they special-ordered everything in—all their appliances, cars, UTVs, shoes, dog sweaters, your uniforms.

They let me clean their bedroom, you'd tell me, hushed about it because you'd signed an NDA. We'd text pictures back and forth and GIFs, mostly about your favorite show at the moment, which was now *Below Deck.* You were avoiding me, but I hung in there with you. You'd send me videos of yourself in front of the TV, watching *Below Deck*. I'm doing this level of service, you'd say into the phone and put popcorn in your mouth with just some of your fingers. You'd point the clicker at the TV.

* * *

Once, I found a handful of Gilded Age books that you had with soft cloth covers. *A Little Maid of Old Maine* is one you'd folded down the corners of.

"'Tis hardly to be believed," a character toward the end of the book declared. "These little maids are brave as soldiers... the Province of Maine will not forget their names."

It's about fighting against the British.

I found another one too, *A Little New England Maid* from 1898. Your bookmark with a particularly tall angel on it was marking a scene where someone in the household asks the maid named Maida (!) how she knows about housework, but the employer interrupts the question and says, "Hush, Maidy has had a chance for a sight of knowledge, with her ma a cripple ever since she was a baby." The end of the page is the character Maida being offended at hearing her mother called a "cripple."

You thought a lot about coming from a long line of women who were maids, who cleaned banks at night or other people's houses in Ohio. I'd watch you brush your hair in the mirror.

You'd hold the little ends of your bottle-blond hair in a curl, thinking. Your mouth lifted up. I know you mulled all this and then located yourself: Fairfield County, Connecticut, home of the *Stepford Wives* and *Ordinary People* and *The Ice Storm* too, right? Unlike your parents, you grew up surrounded by uppity, upwardly mobile families and were supposed to rise up. In the mind of the family, the only way it could have happened for you was to either become Martha Stewart or to marry someone who'd elevate you. This didn't work. Still, you had inherited your grandmother's clean: her sharp hotel folds, her intricate back-and-forth vacuum designs that she'd do in the bank's carpet in Akron.

You became a maid.

* * *

Out there on the dock, leaning over the edge, I could feel my own body being water because that's mainly what it is. After the restaurant closed for the day, I'd go out there to look at the mirror of clouds that was the harbor. The lobster boats were moored for the night and I'd listen to knocking fiberglass being shoved gently around. It was so still that it hummed. Honestly, I was struck with the feeling that being alive was mostly bad. This was the most alone I'd ever been. I'd long craved aloneness, but now that I had it, a boredom was rising around me. I'd come home thinking we could be together, but it was obvious that we were just two bodies in parallel, two buoys tied up and bobbing with no way to save each other.

All of my most relieving dreams are about dying in water.

I dream about Rome like this, I dream about the Hearst pools in Berkley, I dream about hotel pools and docks and slips and one particular Aquatic Center in Saas-Fee, Switzerland. I considered stepping off the dock with a passive exhaustion. I looked out at the green water making rounds against the deep-treated piers.

"Pain makes everything unreal," Anne Boyer says. The world outside my apartment window was a painting. Pain is also whatever. Nobody exactly knows what it is and when I put my mind to it, the sensations scatter or spider elsewhere. I walked home from the dock one day that summer and noticed a throbbing in my side. By the time I lay in my bed that night, it had grown sharper. I told myself that if I still had the pain in the morning, I'd go to the hospital, because it seemed to be at a standard appendix location.

When I woke up, the throbbing was still there, so I walked Bobo around the wharf and put the key in the old Airbnb lockbox on the door because I figured someone else would need to come back to let her out. I drove myself to the hospital imagining I'd get to come right home. The nurses at the front desk were like, it's not appendicitis. You wouldn't be standing. And I was like, that's funny, I can stand but I can't sit. They admitted me but said that because I didn't have a fever or any other symptoms besides pain, they were pretty sure I was pregnant. Two nurses and a doctor separately suggested that I might be and not know it. They shuffled their papers on the small plastic stand that held the computer. They clicked around and seemed so sure that I actually did start wondering. They shot me with that blue dye and put me in the scan tube and it was my appendix. It is the size of two thumbs put together, the doctor said, but it's also way behind your colon and almost at your back, that's why you can stand but not sit. I explained that my grandmother's stomach is in her chest and my family has Ehlers-Danlos, whatever that actually is. He wanted to take it out, take my colon out, staple it all back down. I argued with him for a long time about leaving it, since I had no other symptoms, and he agreed. I had a view of the mountain in my room and I was actually happy to stay. Everyone was very nice. I was in the hospital for four days while they watched to make sure it wouldn't burst, the whole time I was on IV antibiotics and I didn't realize that, at the same time as they were helping, the antibiotics were also sort of snacking on my ligaments and creating tendon damage. Cipro, specifically, is famous for doing this, and that's just how it goes sometimes, I guess.

Like how the bird feeder attracts birds to nest but their spill also attracts baby opossums who attract fishers who kill the opossums in the night with growls that only slightly muffle what are terrifying baby screams shaking through the night.

This is a horrible place, you'd say to me about being alive. You would want to go to heaven because you believed that there was something better than here. Maybe that's why you didn't react when I told you I was going into the hospital. I had called you from the front desk when I was checking in because the nurse wanted to know if there was a family history of appendicitis. You didn't answer even though I called and texted a lot.

The moon was a thin string in the lower lefthand corner of the window near the mountain on my first night there. I guessed that it was setting. A close friend of mine had been suggesting I reframe you as an aunt, so I could enjoy you but not rely on you so much. You not caring whether or not I was in the hospital, in combination with the pain in my body, felt actually unreal. I lay there and thought of how, as long as I could remember, when I hugged you, it felt like you sensed my warmth as a trap and you'd pull away. It is possible that you both loved me and felt trapped. At that moment, a wind shook the glass in the window and I was scared. I need another mom that lives in my mind, I decided. I lay there and imagined one.

* * *

These days, I can't help but constantly go through the things that you left behind. Looking through your little digital camera the other day, I found three or four photos of you and your coworker from the Inn. It looked like you'd invited her over after work because you'd taken selfies of you both playing board games in your uniforms in your living room one early afternoon. This is the only time in your camera and five years' worth of photos that the other person in the photos isn't a date or a dog or Grammy or me.

This camera was one of the only usable electronics I found in your house. You'd died surrounded by broken things. Your car needed new rocker panels and jerked badly when I tried to move it, the batteries were corroded on almost all your devices, your beloved lawn mower wouldn't turn on at all, your lights didn't work, your oven was dead, you were using an air fryer plugged in instead on top of it, how long had you been cooking like that? All your doors were stuck open or closed. I had no idea. Each thing was sparkling clean and exactly in its place.

I once did an interview with Devon Price, author of *Unmasking Autism*, who'd said that he and I have a shared family background, that his dad's side was from Appalachia and were also mixed and made the decision to pass and move to the North. He'd said that the legacy of cultural erasure, and wanting, and uprootedness that's there, we share. His dad had cerebral palsy and his mother made him hide it. There was no job you could do, Devon said, so he hid it his whole life. He didn't take care of his health and died because of that. Then he said of our families: There's this legacy of intense alienation from other people and from yourself.

I spent one afternoon moving all your storage bins from your basement to my house, and one of the heaviest ones was full of diagnostic paperwork. On top was a form from when you'd been to jail in 2016, with *no makeup* circled in red—someone making sure you understood you weren't allowed to bring any.

You'd called me from jail while I was at a new friend's house in East LA having dinner. You had another OUI or something and now you were in real trouble.

Mom, hi, are you okay?

I'd answered from a black-and-white-checkered bathroom at their place after you'd called me so many times in a row. There was a long pause. The longest pause I think you ever made. There were crinkling sounds on the line. I pulled the phone away from my ear to check that you hadn't hung up.

Honey, you took a breath. Honey, I'm so glad you answered. Your voice was hot like you'd been running.

You said, honey, I'm in jail and I might be going to prison. I switched the call off speaker to hear you better. We've just now gotten our phones back and everyone had someone to call but me, you said.

The soft sounds of your crying started. A car engine revved outside. I was silent.

It was horrible, honey, you were saying, I was on this date at the Thirsty Whale and he was scaring me and so I told the bartender and she called me a cab, I know I shouldn't have been drinking, but this is what happened.

You told me you'd gotten arrested for drinking and driving when really, that cab dropped you off at the wrong house, another identical yellow one in your development, and you fell asleep on that stranger's step. When you woke up, you saw your own car in your own parking space at your own house, walked over to it, got inside, turned it on, then backed it straight into this ditch behind you, ripping up wildflowers. Someone called the cops and even though you'd just driven about a foot, it was still your third OUI.

When you went to the minimum-security facility in Warren, you told me you felt like Martha Stewart. You wrote me that you'd be happy to stay in there and keep working on their farm. We wore comfy clothes and there were no men, you'd said. Not even one man that I had to talk to. I feel like I finally had a break.

You know, Mom, Willie and I laughed about this the other day. I went and visited him in Warren, where he is now, the men's version of where you were. I only knew he was in there because I'd gone to Common Ground and I saw a bunch of first-place dahlias from Men's State Prison. We all agreed it had to be Willie and it was. He relapsed about the same time as you did. He's in there for fentanyl.

Around the first anniversary of your death, I got a long letter from him apologizing for not being around to support me after you'd died. He said he loved you and me very much and he'd be really grateful for a visit. A month later, I was down in Warren and we were talking about you getting that OUI in your driveway.

You know your mom was brilliant, he was saying, holding my hands across the table in the visitor's room. Guards in uniforms stood around us.

She was always stuck, though, trying to make sure we only saw this happy side, he gestured in a storytelling way with his fingers all stretched apart. You could tell there was a lot more going on, he said, but she was so talented at everything she did.

I said, I know. It's awful. I wish she could have felt safe to just talk in her baby voice and do crafts and not have to work and everything like that.

The other tables around us had people playing cards. Some of the meetings looked more official than others and many of them were dates.

When I was a kid I used to play this game called bing bang boom, Willie said. He brought his hands in front of him on the table to tell this part. I used to lie on the floor and play with action figures, like really involved with it, and I'd roll around and make noises and it pissed everyone off. My family started to make fun of me, mocking me, so I would hide to play. I think of that now sometimes. Sometimes, I'd still like to lie on my stomach and make noises and roll around. What would it have been like if that was okay, you know? Your mom was like that, she just needed permission to be more herself.

We should be more of ourselves, I think, he said. She was brilliant.

You know, one time she and I were at Little Long Pond, I'll never forget this, he said, and a bald eagle just swooped down and grabbed up a fish right in front of us. She said *shit* or something I think and looked at me with these big wondrous eyes. It was so great. He patted my hand.

I'm so proud of you, he said.

For what?

For loving her through this. You still love her so much and that's beautiful to see.

I love you too, I said.

We held hands together over the table.

When he and I said goodbye, it was to all the sounds of kissing in the room.

* * *

I never gave you credit for how incredible it was that you'd come back from the shame of all of this, you weren't allowed to drive for a long time, so you walked your way to work and you started over. Even one fraction of the strength it took you to return to life after so many incidents like these is more than I have.

Below your carceral paperwork in that same deep Tupperware was a form from a 2019 hospital visit for suicidal ideation. They said alcoholism. Depression. ADHD. Maybe hypothyroid, a restraining order for a scary boyfriend that I vaguely knew about. Then: a self-report questionnaire. *Do you like yourself?* You'd written all zeros. *Do you like how you treat people in your life?* Zero. *Do you like what you see in the mirror?* Zero. Except for one: how you treat animals. You'd circled a four.

These papers are the saddest version of you.

Toward the bottom, under thin yellow and pink diagnosis leaflets, I found a report card with my name. I flipped back through the box and realized that half of the papers were mine, with all the same acronyms listed on them that yours had, ADHD, etc.... and then, at the very bottom were those oldest papers from fourth grade with *retarded* in a red stamp. You'd kept it all, even some email exchange you'd had with my teacher where you said you were in pain watching me struggle in school and you'd asked them to be nicer to me. I think something beyond my child's control is affecting things, you'd said, and this is what I tell everyone about you now.

* * *

Even this Tupperware that I was looking through was almost in shards. Half of its lid was broken into the box. I wish I could have sent this kind of email to your bosses at any of your jobs, something beyond her control is affecting her and she needs a week off, or a few months off even, she hates herself, I wish I could say, and she needs a break.

It's true what Devon said, that you'd developed a powerful alienation from yourself as a response to all the shaming you received for doing things like playing bing bang boom, I'm convinced. When we lived together, you taught me all this as a way to protect me. You taught me to suppress my feelings and distance myself from my body. SlimFast cans were our food. We knelt in front of an empty, whitewashed fireplace and prayed. I was praying for friends. I don't know what you were praying for.

You learned to push your needs down so far that they could only resurface sideways. I knew you to get angry like a door slamming shut on its own loose hinges. I'd hear you moving through the house slamming things and shoving them. Did you need more water? More food? I see it in myself now. I've wanted to press my foot on the gas against this feeling more than once. I've wanted to override it, the way you did.

Tricia Hersey, in *Rest Is Resistance*, insists that capitalism, white supremacy, and ableism condition people—especially those who have been historically marginalized, particularly Black people—to override their body's needs. I see how anger and outburst and violence was sometimes your body's desperate attempt to be acknowledged. You had been taught that stopping meant failure, that hunger was endurance. Hersey urges us to return to fundamental care—not as luxury, but as reclamation. Your self-denial was relentless. This is how I was raised.

Until recently, I wouldn't use the highest setting on my windshield wipers when I needed to and would squint instead. I would sleep in all my clothes. I would sleep very little. I'd drink only coffee all day long or would break a bone and keep at it, just like you. I was stingy.

Last week, I had a meltdown, like the ones you'd have. This is the most embarrassing thing I do. It only happens like once or twice a year but still. Char and I got in a fight about what time we were supposed to start work and I was defensive about it all. I was stuck explaining myself and then overwhelmed. I just want to die, I said and I sprinted to my truck. I knew better, but I threw my phone into the gravel drive so that its face cracked. She said my pants were falling down as I ran with my full strength and speed. I held my pants up while running like a teenager.

These kinds of explosions of feeling have characterized my private life. It's been a forever secret.

Remember when you got ink pen inside the drier at Grammy and Grandpa's in New London and it wasn't coming out of the plastic rim and they weren't back yet from somewhere and you were on your knees crying and scrubbing and I tried to scrub with you? This was one of those times where there was no point in scrubbing because it was so far gone, besides the fact that they probably would have laughed at the stains if they saw them anyway, saying, don't you worry about it.

For you, self-control had a moral value. When these big shows of feeling erupted, we'd suppress them. We'd hide them from each other in the same house and try to tamp things down by drinking. I copied you, and the more I pressed things down, the more unaware I became of the signals of hungry and angry and tired or whatever. I relied on other people needing to pee to know that I should.

* * *

It was the last week of September when you called and asked, for the first time since I moved to the island that summer, if you could come over.

Since my appendix thing in July you'd started to text me again, but if I called you wouldn't answer or would sound weird and hang up quickly. The day before, I'd seen you in the drive through at the bank and the sun shone off your glasses and I could see you were wearing your warmest fleece. I loved you. I said yes to seeing you really fast when you asked.

Through the slider, I saw you in that cream fleece. You were so bright in the light and your smile was sweet right away. I bounced toward you without meaning to go so fast. My body jumped for joy. You had a string of felt things in one hand and a little potted geranium cutting in the other and you were being careful mounting the steps like you weren't feeling too well.

Hi, Mom! My voice seemed to ring around the block. I pulled open the slider.

You looked up at me like I was rescuing you a little.

Your hands were warm passing the felt balls to me. I made these for you my honey, you said, passing me a string of felted Halloween monster faces you'd made and sewn into a garland. I know you love Halloween, you said and I set them down really softly on the tourmaline island.

Oh em gee, these are so good, Mom, wow!

Well, this is so nice, you said, about the apartment.

Thank you, want to see? *She came over* was the thought that kept going on in my mind.

I walked you around for the one minute it took to walk around.

It's so creepy foggy, you said.

Yes, I love it!

Oh, I couldn't do it out here. You rubbed your own arms to say you were scared or cold.

My season's wrapping up finally, you said. So maybe we could go for a pup walk here soon? I got the cat a stroller that I'm really wanting to try out. You touched my arm when you said *wanting* as emphasis like a friend would. I liked that and I thought about it over and over after you left. I'd asked if you wanted tea and you'd said no. I wasn't upset that you'd said no. I strung the ornaments up across the window.

* * *

This was that bright October after your quick September visit. You had a blue hanky tied to your pants' loop and looked stronger somehow than when you came with the Halloween ornaments. Your arms were flexed pushing this stroller that had a zipped compartment with your cat inside, he was a Maine Coon cat from the SPCA, you'd named him Honor Humble Wilderness. We hugged by the little wooden gate after I closed it. Look at him! I said because he was the only cat around in a magenta stroller. He was a gray lump with eyes. He's into it, you said, which was funny. He mewed.

We walked the trail past this boathouse that had hundreds of chunky spiders in every rafter, an open slip in the house for a boat, a boat garage. People were standing in a circle watching their dogs jump off the concrete edge of the boathouse. There were little ghost pipe mushrooms in the tree roots and we didn't make it too far around the bend, just talking and talking the whole time. The last sailboats were going out for the season, tacking toward the wind across from the pond.

Your voice rose. This time last year, I wanted to kill myself, you were saying. Right, I'd said, like we were talking about doing laundry, because this wasn't the first time I'd heard it.

Before I left LA, it was Willie, actually, who'd called me and said sorry about your mom. Sorry for what? I said because I had no idea.

Your mom tried to kill herself, he said, and she's in the hospital, but she's okay, we're with her and he'd just wanted to let me know. None of this surprised me as a possible thing. I thought, she has her cat so at least there's that, she'd never leave her cat here alone.

I just had to wait for the season to end, you said about summer, I was in burnout. You looked at the ground. Your cheeks were red and we were stepping over roots. I was so excited to hear you talking like this. I get it, I said, I've been in burnout too. You walked with a bounce. I found myself wanting to hold your hand.

I asked you more about Salt Cove, which you were excited to talk to me about: their fleet of golf carts, the goose poop in the grass that you had to figure out how to deal with, the specific stone steps that needed a tremendous amount of care. My hurt was waning because, like always, I was enthralled with you. We laughed. Maybe everyone feels like this about their mom.

I want to be buried in that Somesville cemetery, you said then, randomly, but that's historic and there's no space. Wouldn't it be nice to be buried here? You pointed at the wildflowers we were walking past. Dogs bounded everywhere. It was funny to imagine being dead around all the dogs. I don't know why. We rounded the bend, the pond gleamed through the trees.

You stopped to adjust Honor's stroller as a group of labs ran around us. One of them sniffed at Honor but you weren't worried about it and just crunched on ahead. You were a dog person, but you couldn't keep up with a dog on your schedule after your Westie died, you'd said, then there was George, now Honor from the SPCA.

Well, I'm really glad we're here, I said, watching you push the stroller through all the gold light falling around us from being afternoon.

I'm really glad *you're* here, my honey, you said.

At the car, you handed me an armload of puzzles you'd wanted me to have. We could do some of them together, you said, save your favorites and we'll do it this winter on a cozy day.

Aw, Mom, okay, great.

Oh, honey, I wanted to give you this too. You went through your Corolla's consul. I had this in my god jar, you said.

We both had a jar. We'd write down things we were worried about and put them in there, send them off to our higher power. You pushed a little folded sticky note into my hand.

What is it?

Look, you said and nodded.

Help my Em come home, it said, and *2008*.

A car or two went by too close to us and we walked next to the wooden fence away from the road.

Oh, Mom!

Yup, honey, you said. My wish came true! You turned back to your car really quick and sweet. I was MIA this summer, let's try to not do that again this year, right?

Agreed. I said.

And for some reason, my mind flashed to my little-kid handwriting in my little-kid notebook (I was eleven when I wrote this), I wrote, *sometimes I think she hates me and sometimes I think I hate her, but I'd stand in front of a bus for her*.

I'd do it today, I thought, with a bus blowing by on that sharp curve.

Grammy talked like this too. She said when you were a teen, she'd say things like, Marie, you can't have that low-cut dress and go out like that. She would watch while you put on this exact dress that she'd said no to and walk down the stairs trailing your hand on the banister with a cold chin and go out the door. Grammy would watch *Mildred Pierce* forever after that and say,

Veda, that was your mom. She'd shake her head. I didn't know what happened to her to make her that way.

She would always follow this with, oh, your mom and I are going to get doughnuts together tomorrow, or, I think we're going to get pizza on Friday. The feelings were only feelings because we all still hung out and the plan was for more of the fun part, these were going to be our best years, I was thinking.

You handed me *Help my Em come home* and I got back into my truck and pulled my blaze-orange hat low to my eyes. Driving away, I turned the truck toward the little fences and sheep overlooking other islands and the rocky water and I cried driving past it with a quiet heaving. I cried like this every time I left your house or left you. I wanted to kneel in front of whatever it was that stalked you. When we were together, I'd feel you grasping for me. I could feel myself reaching back, but I couldn't fix your feelings like I wanted to, ever. You'd slip from me back into your life, into the knots that held you here. I pictured you trying to kill yourself and I didn't know how you'd tried. I didn't know if you were just thinking of it this recent time or if you were about to. I made my body cold to the idea. I shoved it out of my mind and watched my hands on the steering wheel. I didn't realize it, but I wasn't careful with the puzzles in the truck. I put them in the bed and some of the boxes opened as I drove. Puzzle pieces bright with neon seals and jellyfish trailed out of my tailgate the whole way home.

* * *

I'd felt so good after this, Mom.

That week, I drove to the land near sunset with matches and newspaper and a little axe to make kindling and walked a thin deer path to the place I imagined for a house. It was just beyond the tree line and through a thick meadow. On the trail through the meadow, I found a fox pelt flat in the grass and decided that I'd have my bonfire there. I said thank you to the fox—its small red body that was dried fur and skin—and to all the animals and plants around and to the sun for still being there and to the fire itself and even a thank you to the overturned iron tub and pieces of slate nearby from an old neighborhood pile of trash. I sat in a beach chair and looked toward the tree line. The skin around my temples and my brow had softened and I was smiling easily. I also noticed I wasn't so angry. It's hard to describe, but I felt hugged. I hadn't felt this way maybe any other time besides when I was with Grammy and Grandpa by the sea. How could I go back?

Stars turned up across the horizon line first and then straight overhead. Darkness dipped as a blanket would over some knees and I heard the who-cooks-for-you barred owl call behind me in a large white pine. The constellations were intricate and immense, running with the Milky Way. I thought then, what if I accepted the gift of this? My phone didn't work past the tree line in that meadow, so I felt free. I waited until the fire had died out. Crickets were jumping and crowing and bouncing around my legs as I walked through the meadow back to my car on the street. It was dark. The Milky Way overhead looked purple and I was right in the middle. *I'll stay* was my thought. I think I've decided. I'll stay and I'll build the house.

* * *

By November, rain was coming down in sheets, bouncing off the plastic birdbath in your backyard. A goldfinch and some baby robins were opening and closing their wings in the water, rain hitting their heads like kids. I'd come over to your house to hang out with you. You told me you were back at meetings because you found some online ones in the morning that you liked and the burnout was gone. This was obvious because we were actually able to decide on days and times to see each other. I was spending most of my time in the apartment at work on Zoom and I was the happiest I'd ever been. I would put *Selling Sunset* on the giant TV they had in there and try different recipes with steamed mussels. Grammy says she's never been bored one day in her life and I'd think about that as I looked out the window at the sea, content just to watch the tide crash against the concrete boat launch. For this visit, you'd set up a tray table with a coloring book for me, its edges curling up like the leaves of your geranium cuttings, which were all around your house—windowsills, countertops, the bathroom shelf.

I keep the one you gave me by my bed these days. It's a bush. Grammy has one in her pantry where she goes to sit and talk to you. She loves flowers but struggles to keep things alive at the moment because her hands aren't moving easily. Your geranium is flourishing, though. She always hums the doo doo doo doo *Twilight Zone* theme song when she tells me. This is both funny and very sad.

Where did they all come from? Maybe Salt Cove. You'd stood a box of colored pencils up on the tray table and a can of the fancy soda for me.

Honey, we can watch whatever you want, you nodded toward the TV. I looked for the clicker under myself sort of absently. My phone was buzzing because I had started working with the bank. I hadn't told you about my plan with the house yet but I'd been working on it. I hadn't been able to get the land appraised high enough, so it was suggested that I do things step by step and see if I'd get more money that way. We were putting in a thin dirt driveway in hopes that it'd help, which is what I was coordinating that day.

Things were starting to feel real. I'd gone over there the week before while my arborist friend Charles crouched down and looked up at all the swamp maples, saying, do not touch any of these or the alders or the winterberry. He'd wanted me to put my driveway as close to the neighbors as possible to reduce impacts on the land so that's what we were doing. He'd walked us through the woods to someone's trap shack back there with an oil-drum fire going and we stood around with the fishermen talking for a while because we were about to be neighbors.

I checked my messages and then slipped my phone back in my pocket. Across from me was your red couch from Merrill's, the one Grammy bought for you with its cushions that you'd tried to stuff mattress foam around to keep from sagging. A quilt hung over the back of it for Honor to lie on and look out the window. You'd lined your windowsills with seashells and red candles. Outside, the houses in your development were little matching green and yellow boxes tucked into gullies. It's a rainy day, so *Ghost and Mrs. Muir*? I said.

You got it, you said, which meant I should click on it.

The movie started fifteen minutes in, Gene Tierney was announcing her plan to live by the sea. We put it on and didn't really watch because we'd seen it so many times—it's Gene Tierney and Rex Harrison. He's a sea captain ghost haunting her house and it's a movie about longing, mostly. They can't be together because he's dead, but at the end, she dies and there he is, hand outstretched, calling her by the name only he uses. The doorway fills with clouds, and they finally walk off into eternity. In death, love is infinite like that.

I was hunched over the coloring book, shading in a lighthouse, when a blue blur passed the window.

Sully's here, I said without looking up.

Oh, no way, you said, walking sort of slowly to the door.

His truck slowed in front of the house, idled for a second, then peeled off with tires kicking up water. You stood at the window, hand on the frame, then turned and leaned on the arm of my chair. You picked for a second at a loose thread on your sleeve.

I saw him at the Shell station the other day, you said, your voice mixed with rain. He was drunk and was buying a thirty-rack. He's about to get married again, you said. He was married when we were together too. You hesitated, then said, I'm not proud of that.

It was strange to see that he could make you lower your voice in this way that was unfamiliar to me. Honor lifted his head at the sound of the rain. Gene Tierney was dead now, her hair blowing around her face, walking into the clouds. I reached for the clicker and turned the volume down.

Outside, a goldfinch hopped onto the lip of the birdbath. Water sloshed over the plastic waterfall where your mancala beads slipped around. You leaned against the recliner and I could hear your heartbeat.

* * *

I have the best video from around this same time of you calling Muffina, your favorite red squirrel, who you'd chirp at and she'd chirp back. She was a blush red. You were wearing your pink hat with ears that made you look like a drawing. You lifted off your feet as you chirped.

Your neighbors' kitchens were visible from your window. You'd hung remnants of my early 2000s beaded curtain from Delia's around the new-growth evergreens outside, trying to make curtains for privacy. All you wanted was for me to come sit with you. You wanted to show me your swale you'd dug, the flooding in your yard, the new books you'd found at Big Chicken Barn, your DVR recordings of *Drag Race* and the dog show and *Below Deck.*

From my wharf house, I thought of ways I might support you. I could make you profiles on my accounts. I made a list—Netflix, Spotify, Discovery+. Next to that list was a site plan of the land which had your cabin in the front. I'd drawn another little square and had written *chickens* in it.

Already the wharf apartment was shifting. The light changed to look like winter and moved unevenly through the slider, spilling across the vinyl floor. Some ice was showing up on the water and chunks of it were moving around the buoys outside. I'd see seals bob up around and would try to tell if it was buoy or seal. Each morning for a while it was low tide. Rocks shone in weak sun.

I lit a cedar-and-orange candle from a shop in town and took down the sign that said LOVE YOU TO THE BEACH AND BACK, which was relieving. Why didn't I do that earlier? I only did it because my friend was coming to stay with me. He'd just arrived and was planning to be there for a month, working on a book project and sleeping in this tiny bunk bed in the apartment's second bedroom with the crunchy mattresses waterproofed for children that before him I'd just put laundry on.

You had just texted, let me know when you have room for a visit and are rested for one, with no red heart, but I hadn't responded to your last red heart with one either. I noticed myself counting these hearts like I did with people I dated.

My friend clicked on *British Bake Off* and the tide was high, so we could hear it.

I mean, you deserve to receive love and not just give it, you know? Seems like you're stuck working something out with your mom, he said.

On my way back home that afternoon, I'd passed Willie rambling by in his truck, probably going to clean up *Eden* for the end of the season or for a last sail. I could see he had a patchy beard and looked tired even through his windshield. We hadn't spent any time together in years. I waved at him but he didn't see me.

I had no idea that he was getting in trouble all over the island and I didn't know you were too. I said goodnight to my friend and went slowly to my room. I put on some random Spotify playlist and lit a low tea candle, put it on the carpet in the center of the room. Nothing in the room was mine. It had a small Marden's carpet and a light-wood queen bed frame. There was a TV on a faux-oak dresser and a plush powder-room chair that didn't look like it was for sitting. I lay on my back on the carpet with the tea candle by my ear. One of the refrigerator trucks full of lobster, the last one of the day, rumbled by the window. One had hit the house just a few weeks before, so now I was more alert. The alley was getting older every day.

In what my buddy said, I heard something about how I was supposed to be prioritizing myself over caring for you. I purely didn't know how. I figured I'd learn.

* * *

The air was full of spring somehow but it was still deep winter. All the boats were wrapped and the fountains were boarded in their weird triangle shape and the trees were burlapped but the sun was on top of the porcupine islands like a hallucination. I was waiting for you with my coffee in my hand on the sidewalk because we'd driven from the coffee shop to the bookstore separately. This was a holiday hangout. We had gotten our coffees together and you were so excited. I'd held the door open for you to go creak onto the hardwood floors of this bookstore that we'd been walking into for decades. You had a list of books you were looking for. You'd written down *The Secret Lives of Church Ladies* and *The Little Prince*. I watched you jump for the French-language version. You had sticky notes about it somehow in your hand. I guessed you were working on a project for Salt Cove. It smelled like the pine pillows for sale and the birch incense in there. You smelled good elbowing me and saying, Em, Em, Em, look at this one, holding up *The Secret Lives of Church Ladies*, yes, I've heard that's super good, I said. I'm excited, you said, almost on your toes.

Everyone who worked there and the handful of others inside looked at us. Your energy was bright orange or lemon, ours together was. Everyone always noticed. When we were together with Grandpa, he'd shush us and say, stop, stop, everyone is looking. We got loud and giggly and the cashier was like, I love seeing you two together, you look so much alike, you *are* so much alike. You have the same smile, the lady said and we pointed our smiles toward each other when she said that, which formed a light between us.

* * *

The only time I'd ever talked with you about the land it had been years earlier, when Grammy and Grandpa left the island for

Southern Maine, to be closer to hospitals. You called me saying, Em, I don't understand. They're actually moving. They're leaving me here.

I have something to tell you, I'd said then on the call, I bought land.

Oh, honey, don't get my hopes up, you'd said.

No, I'm serious, we did, I said. I didn't tell you how many acres or what it was like, but I said there was plenty of room for us both and I could build you a house and you could have chickens and anything you wanted.

You responded similarly when I finally said, Mom, I committed to this. I've been to the bank and my friends and I made a plan and I'm building a house. I'm going to live here.

We'll see, you'd said all the way through the whole thing.

* * *

For your birthday that year, you wanted to go on a shopping trip to Shirley's, this craft store you loved. The land was nearby and I really wanted you to come see it because we could now drive on the dirt driveway and that might make it real for you. We'd just finished putting all the culverts in and doing the drive, and

I'd gotten it reappraised and it came out exactly right. I could now build the little house with equity and with no money down. I'd be the general contractor. I was excited to show you the road.

My plan was to drive us up the newly built driveway when we were done at the store and say, Mom, this house is going to be for us, or I can build one for just you too, whatever you want. I imagined you looking around and seeing what I saw and crying maybe. Maybe you'd even say, Oh, honey, I love it, and we'd walk around the cedars in the back.

Shirley's is white sided with a red door, across from the lobster takeout with a giant dancing crab sculpture.

You knew the pink and blue short-haired lady who owned it and waved from the parking lot to her. We had our masks on and you were wearing your pink beanie with the ears and your soft Bean boots. You were saying, I don't think I was meant to be on a planet with so many people. I love that it's empty! This is so fun! I love you, my honey, you said, giving me a side hug in front of maybe Shirley.

We looked at yarn. I paid for yours as a birthday present. I turned to you and said, Mom, I've got something to show you. Are you down to follow me back to your house?

Oh, honey, I have to grab groceries, you said.

You sure we can't just take this left here together so I can show you something?

Next time, honey.

You wanted groceries from across the street at the gas station.

I can go with you and buy your groceries as a present too or we can do it after?

No, no, that's okay! I'm getting tired, you said. We'll see each other soon. You rubbed your eye with your sleeve. Your eyes were just slightly red in the corners. We hugged quickly and I watched you and your pink hat bounce across the street. Cars had to stop for you when you jogged across. Fishermen in tall boots held the door for you.

* * *

I'm sorry I can't come over, Mom, I texted you, we're working on laying the slab today and I'm very tired. What do you think?? I sent a picture of me in a hole, surrounded by bright blue board with the radiant tubing all around that I was trying to install. Okay, honey, you'd said and that's all.

Once building really got going, things moved fast. I'd never done anything as hard, to be honest. I was on the phone almost every day with Hank, who talked me through it all, but still. We put the little pine house under the maples that looked like hands holding it in a way. We didn't dig down to disturb less and it's a little house but is big to me. I'd bought a camper with some of the loan so that my friends could stay in it and help me work. It was extremely fun, truly, but my phone was ringing constantly that summer and fall with things I needed to buy and do. You seemed hurt whenever I got up during one of our shows to take a call about a lumber delivery or something, but I wanted you to just wait for me. I just needed to focus for a little while and then we could craft together and get coffees and take cute walks around and watch bad reality TV. The goal was to have the house done in six months and I was somehow on track but I was teaching on Zoom full-time at two schools and I was wrung out.

You know, I hate any plotline where the characters are at odds, and the audience knows the root of it, but they don't talk to each other about it. I get too frustrated by those scenes as a viewer. I imagine this was going on for you and me, because I could see it between you and Grammy.

When I went over to their place, Grammy pointed at the TV with her thumb and said, I just got your mom a bunch of these. QVC was showing frozen potstickers, fanned out like jewelry. I just ordered her a box, she said on this particular visit, settling into her chair, a bowl of mint gummy candies on the table between her and Grandpa's high-back chairs. I took one of the mint jellies from the glass bowl. The lid chimed like church. Grammy looked out at the water.

We've just done this with your mom so many times, Em, she said and she meant how you'd change plans and disappear from contact, then call them from a hospital, for example. She was feeling you soft-launching another round of distance. You'd begun canceling plans to see them.

I know, I said.

She wiped her hands on the apron spread over her lap. We love her. But boy, does she make it hard.

She makes it easy, and that's what's hard, maybe, I said.

Grammy smiled while looking off. Yes, that's true. We always have a good time together.

We laugh so much, I said.

We sure do, she laughed then.

The Sunday after this, I was with you because you needed me to take some of your bigger trash to the dump. You'd just finished telling me to be careful because squirrels were living in your engine. It had cost you a lot of money to fix, and I wasn't sure what you wanted me to be careful about, since there was nothing I could do while I was parked there for the afternoon.

Grammy seems mad at me, you said, getting hot dogs together in the kitchen.

Sounds like she wishes she could see you more, actually.

I don't know. She doesn't get it. I'm working all the time. She doesn't understand how tired I am. I don't have a choice.

Your Salt Cove uniform was set up by the door for the next day, the polo shirt ironed and on a hanger on the doorknob. You had to work all winter at this job, which was a perk in a way because before that you had to go on unemployment for half the year. Still, you worried about icy roads and not having any time off, but more than anything you were dreading summer. The crush of people was about to come and rest was over, and you hadn't even gotten any. The days were getting longer and you didn't want it. Across from the brown recliners, the TV was on QVC. I had my back to it, but you gestured toward the screen with the point of the knife you were using to cut carrots. The host with a blond bob and chunky earrings was showing the same potstickers. I just ordered Grammy a bunch of these, you said. She loves them.

* * *

We haven't heard from your mom in a few days, Grandpa said a few weeks after that when we'd had lunch. He was worried about you. He came up to me softly while I was sitting on the porch waiting for Grammy to get back from the bathroom. We share the daily scripture reader together, he said, and usually she writes me but she hasn't. He passed me a printout of this scripture he sent you but it wasn't a message thread, it was just a scripture, so I couldn't tell there was no response.

What are you talking about? Grammy asked. Oh, he's worried about your mom, she said to me, that's right. She looked at his printout. I guess it's time for me to call, Grammy said because she hates to reach out. She's scared to bug anybody, so whenever I see her name on my phone, it's serious. You felt the same way, so you answered. I don't know what Grammy said to you or how that conversation went, all I knew was that now Grammy was inviting me over to spend an afternoon as the four of us. She'd made a plan for it to be all of us and laughing as soon as the temperatures were warm.

A few weeks after Grammy's call, we did the almost three-hour drive to their place separately. You and I got to their house within a few minutes of each other. You had that giant feed bag you'd made into an XL purse and I had my enormous red Marden's one. Both of our bags were full of yarn. We hadn't coordinated this, so it was extra cute. Grandpa took our picture with our bags on our shoulders. You brought Colonel's doughnuts and opened the box on the little table by the door. You and Grammy were laughing and talking on top of the sounds of QVC, which was doing hair dryers. Grandpa had a cup of his bad coffee and was trying to go upstairs, already overwhelmed by our noise. Wait, Dad, before you go, you said and pulled a stuffed chipmunk out of your bag. You flipped a switch on its underside.

I love you, Dad, you said.

I love you, Dad, the chipmunk said in a 2X voice.

Grandpa turned red laughing.

Grammy said, oh no, and she rolled into the kitchen, it repeated her *oh no* and now you said, oh no, in your highest-pitch voice and it was a cacophony with the QVC and we were all laughing and the chipmunk was laughing and Grammy said, thank god, because how would we even hear each other without this noise, and now they were onto the subject of vacuum types and we were all interrupting each other and Grandpa said, can you girls at least turn down the TV? because the dog was barking now too and Grammy said, no, Chuck, because we wouldn't be able to hear each other. You were commanding and you snacked on Twizzlers in their plush chair by the TV. My whole body relaxed around you like this.

* * *

Mom, if you, me, and Grammy were memorialized in stained glass like at Saint Saviors, we would be a triptych: Grammy surrounded by succulents and roses and thick, full rhododendrons. She'd be treated by a doctor for something, a man leaning over her knees, her head turned away from him and her hands out, palms up in angry surrender. You would be standing in the woods with a squirrel on your shoulder, your hands raised in arrest, a police car winding downhill toward you. I'd be sitting by the ocean at a school desk, heads of disembodied teachers would make a chorus around me. I would be green with shame, my arms folded across my chest. But on the largest wall, there would be some rendering of the three of us at a table overlooking a beach, you would have your embroidery hoop in one hand, holding the string and needle with the other. Your mouth would be in a slight smile, but also open and talking. Our bodies would be turned toward each other. Grammy would have packets of seeds in front of her, she'd be leaning over and listening to you. I'd have a pencil behind my ear and a notebook out. There would be a herd of dogs in the foreground and, above us, angels who looked like ancestors would have busy wings. The large stained glass would have a gold plaque with an etched title: THE CONSEQUENCES OF LIVING ARE WORTH THE CLOSENESS.

This is what I was thinking about on my drive back after that visit. The tide was high when I got home. I put my yarn bag by the door and pushed through the quiet. I pictured you with the Twizzlers and your fluency at Grammy's, your body's ease there. You and Grammy let your energy sprawl. The sun spilling across the vinyl floor didn't match the cold of that room, but Coasties were hosing off a gun boat under the window and laughing. I hadn't ever been scared in isolation out there, not once. I wondered how I'd feel living further into the woods.

The construction schedule demanded Sheetrock, so I didn't have too much time to think about it. My friend Seffie and I had looped in a Sheetrocker from Florida who was suddenly spending all his time with two trans people and didn't mind at all. We hung on shaky scaffolding on a twenty-foot run up to the ceiling and I pushed myself harder than I ever had. Seffie and I and the young guy would eat pizza in construction lamplight sitting on the scaffold and smile about how fun it was to learn how to build but also how hard. The pieces of Sheetrock were 108 pounds each and we were puzzling them together at arms length above our heads. I wasn't wearing the best shoes. I didn't know it at the time, but I'd hurt my feet irreparably in this frenzy. The frenzy itself was a painkiller, so I didn't notice the pressure I was putting on my soles, stretching the ligaments into shapes they wouldn't return from. This was a small price to pay for home in my mind.

After long days on the land, I would go back to the wharf house and the tide would be out, the boats in their slips rocking lazy. It would be beautiful and almost hurt. The light on the water, the salt breeze coming through the slider, the faint clang of bell buoys would make an inner silence, and without my adrenaline painkiller, my mind would worry. I would turn the worry over and over. Was I being a decent friend to my friends? I'd stress about something weird I said or if I'd talked too much. I would worry that I was taking away a place where deer would lay under the pine. I'd decide I wouldn't make any larger footprint than the house, and I wouldn't let people drive their trucks past this dip in the forest where I saw a partridge once. I wanted to be a good land steward and love the land like family and do all the right things. Could I be a good neighbor to you and a good child? Then I would worry about you and if you loved me or just needed me. How would I ever know?

For all my life, I really believed that if you died and I wasn't with you, I would hear your death inside me like a bell. That it would wake me up if I was asleep. I was the closest person to you and I didn't hear it. Remember that call we had on your birthday the following year? You were crying when I called and I sat up in bed to listen to you.

Mom, Mom, are you okay?

No, honey, I'm not, you said. Please, check on me. I'm so glad you called. I didn't think anyone would. I thought I would outrun it, you were saying, but I'm just like Grammy and Grandpa.

Your thoughts were rushed. I was having a hard time hearing you through your tears.

I spent my whole life swimming upstream from it and it's got me. I tried to keep it out, you said.

What do you mean?

Mental deterioration, anger, isolation... your voice moved closer and then farther from the phone. I look for something I've lost for hours and while I'm looking, I blame people for losing it but there's no one else in my house. Have I lost my mind? It's a genetic thing. Look at your brother, who won't leave the house, look at everyone who we come from who is just like this. I tried to be anybody but them, she said, but here I am. There's nothing I can do. You know Grandpa gave me that genealogy thing from his sister—there were six suicides in there!

Yeah? Six seemed not true when you said it. But Grammy just the other day said that Grandpa's side of the family bumps themselves off.

What do you call that? you asked. You call that messed up.

You can't escape it, Em. You breathed. It's coming for you, and don't ignore me please because I don't have the tools to get you back if you're gone, and I'm sixty and just realizing this and I don't know what else to say.

Your crying was soft and then you said, I have to get to work.

* * *

Mom, I've imagined walking into the sea with rocks in my pockets, I've swam far out and wanted the tide to take me further, I've not put my seat belt on thinking if I died right now in this car that would be fine. I have sort of been waiting for some cool other place to go after dying. Maybe this is deeply entrenched Christianity that I'm trying to unlearn, or maybe it's what you taught me, but I do realize that I've lived with the idea that there's got to be something better than this. I look around at the house I made here and it feels like dying while giving birth. Maybe it *is* coming for me or has come. Maybe it's already here and my door is wide open like with the wind when I moved into the wharf, when I would look at the water and the traps just under the surface and the darkness and how beautiful it looked. I would worry I'd become transfixed like in a fairy tale and go in.

What did you like so much about hope?

* * *

You texted in early May that you wanted me to come over and get my May basket like I knew what you were talking about. I'd just moved into the house. It didn't totally feel like a home yet, but I'd told the wharf landlord on a whim that I needed to move out. I'd told her the house was ready even though it wasn't. Everyone cautioned me from moving into it before it was done but I didn't want to keep paying rent if I had this whole house now. I was okay with breathing mortar and crunching around on crumpled pieces of the Sheetrock in my socks before going to bed, which was what I was doing. But the morning you texted, I'd made my first coffee on my new stove and I looked around at all the tiling I had to do and the light was so soft and perfect coming in through the glass doors and I could feel myself on the threshold of ease. You'd asked me to come over though and I sort of didn't want to go because I was desperately trying to cross this finish line. You said you'd hung a May basket on your front door for me with little paper streamers in there and candy. You said this was something important to living on the island. You had COVID again from work and so weren't coming outside to hug me. I went to your place, relieved a little bit about the boundary of the door because I was rushing. You'd told me recently that it made you cry when your neighbor's daughter would visit her on Wednesdays to check on her. You wondered why I wasn't coming over. Mom, for the first time in my life, I just thought I had forever.

You said we can say hello through the door. I said, okay, Mom, so sorry you're feeling sick, and thank you for my basket!

I could see a little paper cone hanging from the doorknob as I pulled up. You'd laminated the pink paper with a paper handle and paper grass. The basket had some candy in there peeking out and you were in your robe and your pink hat with the ears and you waved at me from inside with those quick back and forths.

I said, I love you, Mom! Thank you!! It was raining. I pantomimed dodging the rain. You laughed and pointed to the basket and I took it grinning and shouting, thank you, Mom! I love you! You didn't open the door, you waved behind it and I returned to my truck, so ready for whatever was next, already unwrapping a Reese's from my basket and popping it in my mouth because I didn't know I'd never see you again.

* * *

Now I have your hankies and your glasses and a picture of us on a shelf above my desk with your little THIS TOO SHALL PASS bumper sticker. I have your socks and your Bean boots and that pink hat. I have your angels and your daily readers and your god jar, I have your birdhouses and your abstract art and your hurricane lamps. I have your CD player and your Taizé CD and the sea chants one. I have your cream-colored fleece.

You only came to the house one time. It was for Christmas, after so many miscommunications about when and where to meet. You were not happy with me.

We hugged and your body was so boney. You had most of your hands in your fleece sleeves. You smelled good still, but your eyes were strained. I showed you this teal camper with nice varnished insides and built-ins and original crystal light fixtures, and said, it's for you, Mom, if you want it, I know you love these. The house is for you too. I put in a second bathroom and bedroom for you and we can also do your own cabin that you can design and build. I said the thing about the chickens.

You looked around and you said, it doesn't get easier from here. The house will need thing after thing.

This broke my heart a little but we went inside and the living room was just dust and concrete besides the woodstove with a fire in it and part of the scaffolding still set up as a place to put things. You got me a fleece from Renys, the microfiber kind I couldn't handle because it almost felt wet on my hands. You'd also gotten me a welcome-home picture of a fireplace and stockings that you'd printed in color, which I lost immediately because I didn't like it very much.

When are you going to come over and get those plates and things?

What plates?

The ones from when your dad and I got married that I've been offering you for a long time now, you said.

Oh, I don't know that I want those, but I'll come soon, I said.

Okay, well, I hope you like your presents, you'd said.

I do, I love them and I love you, Mom.

I love you too, honey. I should go before it gets dark. I can't drive in the dark anymore these days because of glaucoma. I really don't feel good with hypothyroid.

I'm so sorry to hear that, I said.

I walked you to your Corolla and we hugged by your car door. How do you have all these friends? you said, looking around in a hushed way at the group of my friends who were pulling up in a pickup to help with the finishing. I don't know, I said, looking at them. I think it's because I'm trans. You paused for a second with your hand on the car door. I've thought so much about the seriousness of your question. You really did want to know.

I didn't give you any presents at all for the first time I could remember. I didn't ask what you meant about hypothyroid or glaucoma. I didn't try to care for you. I thought, she understands this is the busiest time of my life and it'll all get calm here soon. I just need to get on the other side of this, I'm almost there. After that, I have plenty of time to care for her and learn about these thyroid problems and the glaucoma and drive her to doctors or wherever. You shut your little blue car door and did a six-point turn to leave.

* * *

On August 22, 2022, you sent a GIF with a round pink and blue bunny that said, *if we can be sad for little to no reason… then we should also be happy for no reason!*

This is so cute! I love you!! I said because it was.

The crashing of white walls in the house was wild. I hadn't finished totally everything yet, but the kitchen and the downstairs bathroom were done and the walls were painted and the ceiling was shiplapped. I was just working on the upstairs flooring and that bathroom. There were dried clumps of mud from taping stuck into the corners and the unfinished concrete floor had Ram Board on it in places still, but it was a home.

That morning there were four or so deer just out the window looking at me. They'd slept in the grasses just out front and I could see the goldenrod pushed down around their shapes.

I'd just poured my coffee and was thinking about you, so I texted three red hearts. You responded with a video of your yard zoomed in on your little tiled side table with a bouquet and a little wooden owl. Your video panned over to bulbous white hydrangeas that could be at Martha Stewart's, then up to this four-foot-tall, wild, rotating gem-stoned sprinkler from QVC. Your roses were blooming, your gardening shoes were next to each other ready like a doll's, you showed me your lounge chair, cushions, and some beadwork in a basket next to the lounger. There was also a roll of toilet paper.

In my backyard today, you wrote. Just built my nest in my chair with little things to do… the toilet paper roll is to practice a new fold at work. You sent the crying-laughing emoji and then a pic of a bathroom at Salt Cove with this pursed, scalloped shape made somehow into the middle of the TP.

Kinda hard, you wrote and then sent three red hearts back.

Omgggg your backyard looks amazing and so does the tp! I said. I put the crying-laughing emoji twice, and that was it.

* * *

A few weeks later, it was nearly the end of August and I was putting on a leopard-print button-down. It was velvety. I could move my hand across it and get the fabric to raise up and change shade. My new girlfriend, Char, had gotten it as part of a matching set, a scoop-neck shirt, matching leggings for herself, and this collared shirt for me. She was serious like always when she said I want us to wear our leopard print to Dairy Queen. My arms yawned putting it on. There was a breeze from the south that the trees were smiling into. That second, Char was taking the dogs to the beach at low tide, which was her favorite time to go because the tide would leave emptied out rivets with overturned crabs and fish heads. All of them, all three dogs and Char, would blow back into the house with seaweed stuck in places and the dogs would have eaten a clam or a mussel or something they'd found and she would be kind of sick because of it, so we'd give them a bath and I would be glad when she got in this mess with them actually. She was too. We were going to leave right after she got back and so I was listening for her return. The peace of this moment spread out.

I was happy, like really happy. My cheeks hurt from smiling until there'd be a dip in the action and then I'd think about the fact that you and I hadn't spoken for ten days. We hadn't gone that long since that first summer here. I could feel a clock ticking in my body about it. Char's parents had just left after visiting for the weekend from Quebec because Char and I were now getting serious, a full U-Haul after meeting for the first time in April. I'd thought about texting you that past Sunday when I'd taken Char's parents to the Abby Aldrich Rockefeller Garden with softly cultivated moss. Char's dad squeezed my shoulder as we sponged over pine needles across this garden with monarchs flitting through it all.

Would you like this? Could go either way, I was thinking.

I'd pointed out your block to her parents on our way to the garden. They nodded. Your house was just across the water.

In the garden, I took a picture of these lanky frogs around that rectangular pond. The frogs were laid out on lily pads and everywhere, really big, mouthy ones. I also took a picture of one of the monarchs in the purple thistles and I put those pictures in a text to you. I want to come here with you sometime! I wrote. I sat next to Char in these linen chairs by the pond while her parents imagined every flower in their own garden and I literally hovered my finger over the send button and then I deleted it. I was afraid you'd write back something like, well, that's so nice you have a day off to walk in that garden, I'm here scrubbing floors.

Standing in the sun in my leopard-print shirt, I was thinking maybe I should drive over to your house and check on you like you wanted or sit on your porch. I thought I'd tell Char when she was back. She was driving my truck to the beach in the heat with the chaos of dogs. It was a quick ride, but still. The drive to anywhere was bumpy and dirt. She'd left with a sling around her, the littlest dog wrapped in it. The sun made squares on the upstairs floor. I moved toward the bathroom to look at a new mold stain in one of the windows and I thought, I need to fix that. My mind started in on this stain when I heard some rapping on the glass downstairs. My mind was slow to go toward the sound.

The rapping was loud and the sound also seemed to be moving around. The wall in front of me had nothing on it and I stared at it as if something would materialize. I hoped the sound was a neighbor or something weird that would stop. I didn't move at all. Maybe it's Char. It's Char, I locked her out, I was thinking. I peeked out from around the stairs to the front door. Something brown flashed, then yellow, then gold. It was a guy standing there, his sheriff badge was flashing in the sun. This was a puzzle. The guy was knocking and knocking at the door. I hesitated on the stairs. I watched the guy in his brown uniform standing around, then there was dust. He'd been eaten by it. I stuck my face out further toward the front door. It was dust from my own tires because Char had come up behind him. She was looking straight ahead through the windshield. I watched him shift so his back was to the house. He headed toward her.

* * *

I only answered the door because I watched her coming up behind the guy. I heard the click of his cooling SUV and Char talking to him. The dogs were all getting tangled. The guy was pointing at the house. Char's face wasn't moving at all. Then they both turned toward the door and I was right in their line of sight. I saw their eyes light on me. The dogs jiggled. Char and the sheriff stopped and then started again toward me more clearly. It hit me that Char was trying to cover for me, not knowing what the sheriff was there for. The guy had no one with him, which seemed strange. His SUV was off. Nothing was flashing or blinking. I made myself lean on the door as I opened it like on TV so the set didn't move. I didn't know why I did that. My heart was pounding in my hand. He wasn't standing in the square way they usually do. He was turned slightly with his hat in his hands. The sun screamed off his black shoes.

It can't be about Mom, I was thinking. It can't be you. You seemed to be doing okay. But it occurred to me that you must not have been, actually, because I'd just put your name in the search bar of the police blotter a week earlier to see, in the softest way possible, if anything had happened. There was that new sort of silence from your house that I could feel. Were you in the hospital? Would police come for that? Maybe jail? I started thinking *please*. I thought it so loud I imagined it had come out of my mouth. The sheriff noticed my hand holding the door and he pointed through me to ask if there was somewhere we could go sit down. Now my body was shaking because endings go like this. I don't know what Char did with the dogs. They were gone. I sat in a chair in the living room in the sun. Char sat on this footstool so she could be close to me. As the guy was sitting, he was saying, I'm sorry. Looking up at me with his hat still in his hands, he said, your mom has passed away. Char squeezed me involuntarily.

I said, okay, and leaned forward in my chair to emphasize that he should leave immediately. My whole world was making a tilt and I was sick with it.

Char got me some water.

A calm panic made its way to my face. There was nothing to do but my body found panic.

Did she kill herself? I asked.

He nodded and again he said, I am sorry.

I asked if there was a note and he said, just a piece of paper with your name on it that told us to come here. He said, what would you like me to do with the cat?

I was thinking he meant an alive cat, so I looked at Char, because of the dogs, and I opened my mouth but she put her hand on my arm. He meant the cat died too.

Did she die with the cat? I asked them both and he said again, what would you like me to do with its body? I don't know, I said.

And my grandparents know, right? I asked and he shook his head. I don't remember who this man is at all. I wouldn't recognize him or his name. No, he said, we've just told you.

He saw the nightmare in my face and started to ask if I wanted him to call everybody but I said no, even though that would have been nice. I was scared of Grammy and Grandpa talking to the police. The amount of shock in my body was toxic to me and I didn't want them to feel that. They'd been hospitalized in the last year for heart problems, both had separate heart surgeries in the spring, they were eighty and eighty-five years old. I'd just helped Grammy pick out a card for your birthday that said, *You're so lucky when your daughter is also your best friend.*

I asked if anybody had closed your front door. I think so, the sheriff said and it wasn't reassuring. I couldn't imagine that you wouldn't leave a note. I lost the thread of my thinking so quickly though because the room started to feel small and I felt larger and larger in it. I'd never felt that before. It was almost like I was leaving. I looked for you in the room and then in my body.

I didn't want to hear the guy anymore. He kept asking if I needed anything. Char helped the exchange end. I wanted it to end before it started. It wasn't ending and it wasn't ending and everything was over.

Out the window, I watched him catch his hat down the driveway because it was pushed around in some wind.

* * *

Do you remember when we'd go to Sam Moon in Dallas, that wholesale place for purses and rings and stuff, and you were so excited and I'd get something covered in plastic diamonds—like a T-shirt bedazzled fully—and wear it to match some sandals you got with the same chunky plastic rubies? We'd go back to our duplex as disco balls.

Do you remember when you'd take us to Dinosaur State Park and listen to the T. rex song and then put our footprints in the dinosaur footprints and we'd be there so early in the day with no other kids and a mist would rise up from the limestone in a Cretaceous way and you'd hold my hand to run back to the car in a downpour that would make it so we had to sit for a while in the parking lot because you couldn't see?

When the cop left, my body gasped like falling off a boat. I was remembering a thousand things all at once. I would have texted you about these memories and the clouds that were coming up from the southwest. It was dark out in the day because of them. We were driving to your house because I didn't know what else to do and neither did Char.

Char asked me if I wanted to pull over to look at the clouds and I did want to. I took ten photos of the light that came from under them. She was being so calm.

Did you make your own death? I guess you can only make your own death part way, like how a body goes to bed and waits for sleep.

There's nothing like this. Your front door was closed. Your car was pulled up like normal. The beads I'd gotten you, multicolored glass beads that you'd wanted for Mother's Day some years before, glittered along the little gravel walk where you'd put them. Nothing was locked. A rain started that drowned out much of my thinking. Your smell was everywhere. The feeling of your body moved me around the living room. Those clouds were all across the sky, keeping it dark. I peed in your bathroom by the front door. Mom, I just kept saying, Mom, what happened? Tears filled my mouth.

Your little table with a lamp was by the bathroom next to the front door, you had red and white little felt balls and paper hearts hanging above the windows, a painting of Bar Harbor with sunset colors that I didn't love, a stuffed snowman on the couch and cat toys in the corners of all the furniture. The room was in a weird configuration, you'd turned everything on an angle so the TV was sort of by the back door and then your craft table and rocking chair faced that. You had many angels. Angels everywhere really, and hanging paper hearts above this altar you had with starfish and your god jar on it. There was nothing on any of these surfaces, nothing addressed to me. And then I noticed what looked like a traffic ticket sitting on the corner of your kitchen counter. I walked over to it and held it up to the kitchen window to see better. It said, *theft, August 25* and *theft*. Under that were handwritten notes from you to yourself. *7 p.m. meeting? Call D.A., priors*, it said, you'd circled and underlined many things. You'd been arrested, it looked like. I thought maybe this had to do with your job at the estate. Maybe it was a big deal? Like had been going on a long time. There was no clarity in the summons. Just *theft*, it didn't say the location or anything, and even the word *theft* was hard to make out. Your handwriting was clearer to me. You were scared in these notes and thinking so fast.

Char was upstairs while I was looking at this. There was nothing amiss anywhere except the strange room configuration downstairs, but everything else was just the same besides smoke-detector batteries left on the stairs like someone had dropped them. I wasn't sure if you had taken them out or if the police had. I think probably you did. On your basement folding table there were the manuals for the smoke alarms and for the generator. You had sticky notes on them with instructions on how they worked.

There's no note in her room, Char called down to me, I walked up the stairs to join her in there, but she was coming out, pulling the door behind her. I don't think you need to go in there, she was saying, I think you shouldn't.

But there's nothing?

I figured you'd have left a note by your bed or in a drawer that they didn't see. Nope, Char said, and was like, can you just not go in there yet?

Okay, I'd said, sure, and turned away to go look somewhere else.

What Char saw inside your room was your sweater on a pushpin by the door. I guess you hung it there every night. Your slippers. The generator. A robe on the floor of your closet mixed up with other acrylic blankets and things. Your little blue clock, and the warm soft tissue of your body that had sloughed off onto your bed.

It occurred to me as we were looking around that I had no idea where you were. You weren't at the door waving to me with an innocence that crashed into pieces. The last time I saw you there was through the door and we didn't even hug.

I became frantic to outrun this. Your purse was by the door with Mentos in it and small notes to yourself about things to do for work. I put this on my arm. You had a laser for your cat in there too and that was it. Your phone kept buzzing, I had that also. I didn't want it. It was locked and I couldn't get in. I learned after trying passwords all night that if you do that it gets locked forever.

* * *

This is what happened: sometime between August 29 and August 31, you filled a red Honda generator that Grandpa gave you for power outages with the special mixture of gas and oil that it required. You spilled some of the gas onto the basement floor when you poured it. You had to make that mixture for a few minutes at least and as you were preparing it, you were encircled by large storage Tupperwares of our childhood drawings and toys mixed with an upsetting hodgepodge of family photos in frames that had been displayed at some point in different houses with different combinations of husbands and boyfriends—kids' faces were sticking out of these clear plastic storage bins. Around these was another ring of storage shelves, this one full floor-to-ceiling with survival gear, food pellets and canned goods, dry goods, even a storehouse of maple syrup and some cookbooks. What were you imagining living through? A power outage or like large-scale famine? I'd never seen stockpiled human food pellets before. There was a tremendous amount of water stored. For what? You were about to die.

You lugged the forty-seven-pound generator up the two flights of stairs from your basement into your bedroom. In order to do all this, you had to bump past these little felted balls you'd made and had sewn little beads in and hung on your stair rail as a reminder to pray. You'd hit them and say prayers. One of your prayer balls had detached, either in the process of bringing the generator up, or the part where they carried your body back down. You had a bag of empty can redemptions on your basement stairs, ready to go out, and your laundry hung up on a little line across your washer and dryer. You had a calendar full of things, you'd even written in a camping trip for yourself in September. You had your coffee cup, a container of trail mix and a cheese stick ready where you kept it to go to work the next day.

I'll never know your interiority in this moment. It's one of the worst parts of this whole thing. Everyone speculates, were you angry? Were you rushing around or slow and lonely? In your bedroom, you set the generator on the floor blocking the drawers to your little yellow hand-painted dresser, then bent over, and pulled the generator's ignition cord like a lawn mower. You took off your small black slippers and you got into bed with Honor. I wonder if you called him in there or if he came on his own.

Your windows looked out onto the backyard that you'd meticulously cared for. I don't know anything about what happened next except that the exhaust must have begun to fill the room. Did you cough? Everything in the house still smelled like this exhaust and spilt-gas mixture and the death of your body which really just smelled like very strong dust. Did anything in you try and stop it, like did your hand come to your mouth or your eyes? There were two windows in your room that you'd shut and locked. You had that small blue analog clock that you'd taken the batteries out of in front of your little TV.

I didn't ask the people from your job what they saw when they went to do a wellness call on you after you hadn't come in for work for two days. I do and don't want more details. Did you have earplugs in or the radio on? Your radio was by your bed on the classical station, it was unplugged when I eventually went in, but maybe the police did that. Did you have any thoughts at all? Your bedroom door was closed and the room was filling with smoke. Did you talk to God out loud? Were you distressed or euphoric? You died under your intense Jesus on the cross that Grandpa gave you hanging above your bed. Did you think of us at all? My brother's painting of a bridge with abstract lily pads hung next to the Jesus. Your whole house sighed and then that echoed.

* * *

I'd picked up those frenzied notes to yourself that you had on the counter with the ticket and your lists of phone numbers written on one corner as I was pacing around. I was back to your place the next day and every day after that. Your handwriting was slippy and raw and it was clear you were thinking and writing and making decisions quickly.

I don't understand, you'd written down the margin of one page.

I looked harder at the paper and I called the sheriff's department. I said, I'm hoping you can tell me what happened. They transferred me somewhere. I could hear a person clicking around and looking something up. I'm so sorry, can you hear me? the person said. Your mom was summonsed for stealing sixty dollars' worth of merchandise from Walmart on August 25th from the self-checkout.

I was pacing upstairs in your craft room when I called. This was the room we'd spent the most time in together and my body had wandered up there on its own while I was waiting on the phone. The light was flooding in from the south and falling on these boxes you had stacked against craft supplies. I'd been looking at them and when the person said sixty dollars, I realized I'd absently opened a box on top with Dior printed in gold on white. It was empty aside from some tissue paper.

Everything made sense immediately. The one below that was Hermès in orange with a loose ribbon. There was YSL and more Dior. The empty boxes were from Salt Cove. I don't know if you snuck them home or if they let you keep them. You died because of getting caught at Walmart. Maybe you were in the self-checkout and had to pee and just needed to leave or you'd seen a scary ex-boyfriend somewhere and were going too fast or maybe you'd made a mistake and didn't count right or maybe you did it all the time.

I said thank you to the person on the phone and my body folded. I was in a squat with my head in my hands around the loose tissue and empty designer boxes.

Your arrest would have come out in the police blotter. We read those every week: so-and-so was arrested for theft at Walmart. Cops & Courts comes out on Wednesdays and everyone in town reads it. I stood up and typed your name into my phone again like I had a week or so earlier. There it was: your name, age, and theft. It didn't say the amount or where but this would have been enough for you to lose your job.

I didn't know you'd crawled under the house to die. I didn't know so I didn't go over there to make you laugh and get us back inside.

* * *

Immediately, my grief for you was particular, like sun shining off money on the ground. In sharp focus, I pictured you polishing millions of dollars' worth of art every day, walking past perfect gardens, the high-bush blueberries and rhododendrons leading to an embankment and then the sea, and thinking it was some fault of your own that you didn't have paths blanketed in pine needles or lined in blueberry sod.

I used to teach Laura Gottesdiener's *A Dream Foreclosed* about the housing crisis in 2008. Gottesdiener interviews dozens of people who'd been targeted for predatory loans and eventually lost everything. Nearly every single person who'd been targeted blamed themselves.

But the loans were predatory! my students would yell. They were trying to trick people, so why did everyone think it was their fault?

I'd get chills in the classroom when this happened. My students were all at once recognizing how violent the system is and how effective shame is at hiding it.

I feel sick thinking about you being detained in that concrete-walled back room of Walmart, grabbed up by police at the end of the self-checkout. The fear in your chest! You were snapped up by people paid to guard things mostly working-class people buy, manufactured in exploitative ways harmful to infinitely more people all over the world, while this one particular family becomes one of the richest to ever exist.

Meanwhile, you'd been led to that back room by police with people turning their heads. Then you had to drive yourself home. You had to drive past my block, where I was having a great day in my new house, past the Trenton Bridge Lobster Pound with its smokestacks going on the bridge, past the mussel boats, and the billions of dollars' worth of estates tucked into the trees, you passed all that and didn't stop to get anything at the Town Hill Market, I bet, because that was only for a treat when you were feeling good.

You parked the Corolla, went inside, didn't tell anyone at all, tossed the ticket on the counter, and tried to figure out what to do next on paper. You hung your head.

* * *

After learning all this, every night after for the next year or two I'd wake up at 3 a.m. in a tangle of dogs next to Char in extreme pain. In one of these late-night sessions of looking at my phone, not able to fall back asleep, I found some statistic that if your parent kills themself, you're one hundred percent more likely to die that way. The heartbreak was so supreme that it felt like a vacuum. Regret was thriving in me.

Three weeks before you died, I was driving Char past the Shell station between your house and mine and you were there. I saw your bleached hair and your cream flannel and I was like, oh, there she is, that's my mom and tears welled in my eyes as we drove past you. The two of you had never met, so I pointed you out. Char was like, what's making you cry? and I just said, I love her so much. I'm looking forward to when we can really connect. That was it, then we drove past Pirate's Cove mini golf and I started talking about that instead.

* * *

You know what? I woke up this morning and it snowed. For the last two days, rain had melted several feet of ice and turned everything that was clay and sand into mud. Just as it was beginning to seem like we lived in a drowning world, the ice snatched things up and the maples started running, the snow blanketed everything. It was a kind of relief, a respite. We are in suspense of spring. But this freeze-thaw is the kindness of a gentle transition like loving someone who you know is dying.

I didn't experience this with your dying, it was all flood. It happened so suddenly that shock was my pervading emotion for a long time. When you died, nice people trying to help wanted to tell me about their own experience with parent death, mom death, but I only wanted to hear from people whose parent died suddenly. How did the person survive the shock is what I wanted to know.

I would be talking with anyone about anything then I'd remember: a sharp cramp would bloom into something unsurvivable.

Why did you leave me here? I've screamed at full volume, seeing a blue Corolla in my rearview on my way home. And yet, there are times now, years later, where I can't recall the pain of losing you totally. Maybe this is my own body doing the freeze-thaw thing on my behalf. In these blank-spot moments I try to remember what it is I want so much and it's you, me, and Grammy, together.

With you and Grammy, I didn't have to explain myself. Everything turned funny, and we laughed until our stomachs hurt. I think about that metal porch table with the plastic cloth where I'd sit with you guys and feel so grown up. I was always still real young.

I went down to Grammy and Grandpa's house the other day and Grandpa, who is eighty-eight and ailing, needed me to make his bed. There were a few small spots of blood on it. I lingered over those blood spots like a warning. I've almost never been in his room. I noticed his god jar under the painting of that sailboat on

Assawaga. These are his treasures. The god jar is the only other thing by his bed besides a beautiful teenage photo of Grammy. You'd made the jar for him with a decorative jelly label that you'd drawn on, encouraging him to put notes or prayers in there. I wondered what he'd put in there but I didn't touch it. His health maybe.

He said the other day not to be worried about it because people know when it is their time.

I wondered if he was talking about himself and you.

On their round table by the stairs, they've made an altar to you. The photos are of you at all ages, some sweet '80s ones in a tropical-print hat, others where you look caught on camera and stark, and then some kid ones of you holding your elbow loose on the deck of a boat. You could walk right out of them and back into the room.

Your face moves through mine. I resemble you. So where did you go, exactly? If I am the most of you still alive, does that make me the place you live? Physically, we're not so different. Our hips, our jaws, the way we hold a fork or turn our head when we're thinking—it's all so close that it confuses time.

Before your dying, I used to want success or something but now all I want is calm, a pervading calm.

Roland Barthes writes about this in his *Mourning Diary*, a book of notes compiled after the death of his mom. He writes about how he notices a totally different feeling after she's died. He no longer cares about posterity and writes of a "complete acceptance of vanishing utterly, no desire for a 'monument.'"

He can no longer bear traveling. "Why is it that I keep trying, like a lost child, to 'get back home'—though maman is no longer there?"

I relate so much.

Before this, I was working toward being interesting and cool—at least, in my mind I was. I thought so much more about what people thought of me. The approval I was seeking in others was maybe your approval, which I guess is a standard thing. You'd warned me forever about not staying in the house like Grammy, the value of trying to have friends and being *out*. I'd been letting go of this performance for a while in little ways—leaving the city, being more honest with myself about what this body needs—but your death slammed the door shut on my performing entirely. I've put up a cattle gate a few yards from my house and I want to stay inside it forever with the dogs and your ashes.

"The locality of the room where she was sick, where she died, and where I now live, the wall against which the head of her bed rested where I have placed an icon—not out of faith—and still put flowers on a table next to it. I have reached the point of no longer wanting to travel in order to be here, so that the flowers will always be fresh," Barthes writes.

I went all around the world to be interesting. I got degrees as a middle finger to everyone. I wore all black and partied. But at the end of the day, here I am with an ocean special interest and a pain that's so familiar the only way I know it is as "sleepy" and I'm sleepy all the time. It feels better to be this sleepy in the woods and by the sea.

Right now, all the culverts around me have their mouths wide open with water pouring out. It will all freeze again for sure. The moss is making patches of green, and fog mixes with everything. I look through the fog for signs of anger. I can't find any toward you. There's anger all around us. People are pissed at you for taking yourself out and not explaining it. We wanted a love letter to ourselves. We wanted you to acknowledge us, but I don't know what it's like to end my life and it must be a different sort of state where holding a pen is unreal.

* * *

This was Grammy and Grandpa's first time in my house and I was grateful we'd just finished putting in the ramp. Grammy wheeled into the living room and Grandpa stood. The light from our glass doors was supreme. No one was crying.

The sun bounced off Grandpa's glasses so I couldn't see his eyes.

Charline, they were saying. We're so sorry you're having to be here for this. Welcome to the family. No one was laughing. Grandpa sat finally in my square chair and his tall, curly-haired self folded his palms in his lap, then put his hands between his thighs and pushed his thighs together so his feet were now out wider than his knees. His Velcro shoes looked soft.

Where is she? Grandpa asked about you. He was suddenly a little kid.

I uncharacteristically cleared my throat.

I told her so many times to make a will, Grammy said. She was in her sweet, thin blue pants and her white sneakers with tall socks. She had a nice sweater on. Her engagement ring that matched her eyes flashed in the sun. And no note, huh?

I shook my head, they said no and I've been trying to find anything because that doesn't seem right.

Do you think someone killed her and this is all… she shook her head and looked up at me like a rose.

I mean, I don't, but I guess…

Grammy continued, she was supposed to come over tomorrow for doughnuts. We were going to spend the weekend together, she said. Why would she…

Grammy paused and looked down, she couldn't even say as much as an *I love you*. I don't know, Em. What happened?

None of us got up or spoke.

This isn't real, Grammy said, how could it be?

* * *

May, your next-door neighbor, was standing with her hands on her hips at the end of your undifferentiated driveways. I'd heard so much about her but had no picture in my mind. She had shoulder-length brown hair and a sure face.

Char was standing by my truck waiting for the cleaners specializing in unattended death to get there. Char had asked that I wait to go in your room, so I hadn't. This was the day I could.

I found your Walmart receipt on your kitchen windowsill, August 25 for sixty dollars (I guess they made you buy it in the end, I don't know.) It was mostly food and I think a moisturizer. I would have bought you anything. I was walking over to May with your little blue handkerchief I'd found in your coat pocket in my hand.

May had motioned for me and then stood wide-legged as I walked over.

Hi, I'm Marie's kid, I said.

I shook her hand.

She shook her head.

I'm sorry, she said.

Yes, me too, I said, very much.

Your mom and I didn't always get along, she said.

I nodded. A couple of crows flew around.

She was a little... May tilted her head and made a little click with her tongue. I narrowed my eyes to look at her. She shook her hand back and forth on its side to indicate she was a little, like, loose in the head. I felt a heat move into my hands.

But she seemed to intend to see me last Sunday, May continued. She said a very serious hello to my sons and they were like, how weird, it was like she knew... May said, gesturing toward Mom's house. She never really talked to us, not like that. I've been telling them all the time that what happened to Marie is a good example of why...

I cut her off. The heat from my hands was now in my throat and my chest.

I wish I'd have gotten to see her on Sunday, I said, I'm jealous. Well, thank you for any support you've given to my mom over the years. I turned away.

I wasn't interested in hearing your life refracted back to me through her experience. I was afraid she was going to say something like, that's why you have to be friendly, otherwise you'll end up like Marie. I was afraid to hear her talk about you in an ableist way. I don't actually know what she was going to say. I was jumpy. I didn't want you to be misunderstood, which was a feeling you'd worked so hard to avoid in life. You are a hero to me, like this. You'd warred against surges of shame for sixty years. Everyone I know steals from Walmart! I stopped myself from saying this to the sheriff when they told me what happened. I wish I could have told you that. I wish you'd have called and said, Em, I need your help. You didn't do anything wrong, given these conditions. I saw you as gallant. It seemed that no one else saw you that way. I was wishing desperately for a note, for any kind of recognition of your love, a final sort of acknowledgment of me as your compatriot in this.

A few days later I got a frantic call from Grandpa asking why there were now police at his door.

They wanted a DNA sample from Grammy and Grandpa. He was scared that something weird was going on. When I called to figure it out, the medical examiner said you weren't identifiable, which none of us could understand.

Because of the heat of the generator, the rate of decomposition was much higher than if she hadn't been in there with it running, he'd said. She was at a very high rate of decomp when we found her. He paused because he was trying to tell me that your body melted like a candle.

Summer was going on without you, peak summer.

* * *

I have your worn, gummy tortoise-shell glasses and I have that little porcelain house which opens as a kind of charm box you'd kept on your dresser, it says *hotel* on it. There's a white twenty-four-hour chip inside, the camel chip that says *the tasks of the day can pass with ease when a camel or I start on our knees.* There's also a little ruby pin that says *excellence in housekeeping*—your treasure from the Bar Harbor Inn—and three porcelain figures: two tiny chickens and one farmer, hands holding the bib of her overalls. All of this lives next to a little candle that I change whenever it burns out. It's now been three years.

I have everything you owned in the attic of my house and some of it in a storage unit in Ellsworth still—that new one by the Dunkin, which is very fancy and pipes in those awful static sounds to prevent people from sleeping in there, a particular kind of evil, right? Tyler pays for the storage unit, which is nice of him.

We still haven't gone through your hope chest together, so in some ways, it doesn't feel like we've gone through anything at all. It's in the storage unit around all those Tupperwares from your basement that are full of Legos and robots and puzzles that maybe Tye and Gunner want in case they have kids.

I did open the chest on my own after the unattended-death people came. I marched away from May and went straight upstairs where I knew you'd kept it, under that south-facing window with your little doily curtains.

Every time I see your handwriting, it's like I've been lit on fire. I love seeing it. I hoped that opening the hope chest would make everything make sense, but what was in there was just weird. Under a random, worn-out Trump yard sign, you had a handful of my books that I didn't know you'd bought. They were stiff, unopened. In a manilla envelope, there were letters to Hank about trying to save your relationship. VHS tapes of you on *The Home Show*. Loose school pictures of you and all of us. My childhood intelligence tests fanned out and strewn near the bottom.

There were some of our baby teeth in little red heart boxes and an envelope of hair from my first haircut on top of the baby books.

I closed it annoyed with you because it was more like a time capsule that I didn't care about. I wanted to know what you were thinking. I didn't care about political yard signs from the neighborhood.

Later, once we'd moved everything to the storage unit, I sighed before opening the chest again. I wanted to bring my baby book home with me, so I was fishing around for that and got fixated on this picture of you as a third grader that looked like me. When I picked it up, a note in your handwriting fell off the back and fluttered to the floor.

Do I have autism? it said. *Is that what's going on?*

I stared at the sticky note on the low pile carpet of the storage unit.

I didn't know that you'd even thought about having autism. I reached down and picked up the note. This was your message to me in a fogged-up mirror. For a while you taught talented and gifted classes in elementary school and you'd taken seminars on autism and neurodivergence. We talked often about how Grandpa, who says hello by handing me a printout of something he's been researching about my car, for example, would have met the criteria if it had been something more known back then. I'd never heard you include me in this, or yourself, even though it was floated about me at different points in school and was likely my reason for being in special ed, though that was always vague.

I realized now that all along you'd been wondering why you were so tired after every social interaction, why you would put your fingers in your ears if someone was chewing nearby you or opening something in a loud wrapper, why everything was too bright or too strong smelling, why you'd developed a household concept called "departure time" because transitions were hard for us all, with a system of egg timers and rewards, why you were obsessed with routine but also struggled to follow it, why you watched the same shows over and over and only one or two channels—this is a family trait for sure, just the Weather Channel, QVC, or Hallmark was always on—why you were prone to outbursts and meltdowns and burnout and why you mostly wanted to study what was interesting to you and to play rather than do anything else.

These are all things I do too.

I could see suddenly how I was connecting to you across time and space whenever I unearthed my childhood blanket, for example, and walked around the house in it with no care at all for if it was too immature. I could twirl the little heart-shaped buttons that you'd sewn on there with my fingers and pace around if I wanted. I did this anyway because I couldn't help it, but I no longer had to imagine *helping it*. Even better, I could be with you when I was with me like this.

The first thing I'd heard in my head after the sheriff had left that afternoon, while Char was getting the keys for us to leave for your house, was a whisper from the red maples overhead it seemed.

Honey, I am your mom like the sky is a blanket. I heard this in my head or through the wide-open windows, I couldn't tell. I couldn't do the best job of being your mom while I was alive, but I can do it now and I will. I'm right here, honey.

It was raining out. I could see the rain through the glass slit in the door of the storage unit. I might consider sleeping in here amid you as papers were it not for these piped-in sounds, which I know is the point.

I picked up my baby book.

It was musty smelling but only slightly. The book is from the late '80s, with a Marie-Madeleine Franc-Nohain drawing of a baby in a bassinet. The baby's hand reaches up gently on the cover, it has a washed blue background and a deeper, less-washed blue spine. I put your sticky note about autism on it and as I was about to close the chest, I was filled with something that was, I guess, hope—that spaciousness of uncertainty—and I haven't opened it again.

* * *

How do I tell you this? As an adult, I wanted to stop the self-punishment that we had learned together. When I was in my mid-twenties, I'd gone into the counseling center at my grad school to try and get some help with this. It was an open space with little kiosks that had some trans flags on them and mini flags of different countries, and the people coming in and out of the offices all looked so young.

I saw my friends walking by with coffees, they were going to see something in a gallery that was cool. I was reading *IQ: A Smart History of a Failed Idea* by Stephen Murdoch, and I was learning how fixed intelligence tests descended directly from eugenics. (Francis Galton, who coined the term "eugenics," believed intelligence was fixed, heritable, and measurable and that it should be used to shape the population through selective breeding. His ideas laid the groundwork for Alfred Binet's intelligence tests in French schools, which relied on culturally specific idioms familiar only to Western Europeans. In the United States, these tests were fashioned into tools for ranking kids and creating a hierarchical selection system.)

I was also walking around with a printout of Renee Linklater's work from 2010 and I sat with a sunny window behind me warming my arms while I waited, reading about how Linklater believed the Western therapeutic project and colonization made it so that people are forming our identities and whole cultures around these diagnostic labels—depression, anxiety, ADHD, autism—because there's nothing else like shared culture or spirituality to group around.

When the person opened the door to call me into this intake place, I dropped my books. I was struggling to get my books off the floor because they were doing that strange suction thing that sometimes flat things do on a flat floor. This was funny, so I was laughing and fumbling and I spilled some coffee on that institutional carpet and on my book, but it was busy in there like a bullpen and no one was laughing or looking at me. This counselor person was standing with her arm toward her open office door the whole time. We were probably the same age.

I sat down on a couch in that soft darkness and crossed my legs at the ankles. I'm wondering if I can do an autism screening, I said.

Yes? Do you want to talk about what's going on for you?

Well, I'm feeling frustrated that the only screenings I ever did which landed me in special ed when I was a kid don't actually help me as an adult, they were weird drawing ones—like the

Draw-A-Person test which I did really badly at, I said. I do feel like diagnostic terms are our current cultural metonyms, the ways we try to name aspects of ourselves that can be challenging but also really beautiful...

I was talking quickly with a dedication to accuracy for no real reason. Anyway, I trailed off. Overall, I feel very, very stressed when I can't get something right, I said.

She was nodding and saying, well, I can give you referrals for a screening, and immediately I was like, this is not a thing that I'll ever do. Maybe if it could've happened right there in her office I'd have gone along, but I didn't really believe in diagnosis anyway—not when, like Linklater says, it comes out of a colonial system that breaks a person into parts and is weaponized. Still, it can help sometimes to have language for what's happening, a way to describe a cluster of things that otherwise just float around unnamed. But the moment getting support means calls or forms or waiting lists I feel myself slip out of it, like I always do. "Inaccessible" is a word for this. It occurred to me that I also only wanted help if I could have it for us all. I think my whole life, I felt that I owed you my discomfort. I don't think you intended for me to feel this way.

"I think we can help make the social and cultural conditions so that more and more people figure these things out and find us," Price continued in that interview.

I've lamented this endlessly: why couldn't we connect on these subjects while you were alive? I was sitting in the kitchen looking at your ashes the other day and in sorrow, outside of my control, my body folded face down into the table and I seized with tears. I cried into the table with all the dogs licking my legs.

* * *

I've been watching *Survivor* (season 48, I don't know why Char and I are watching it, neither of us has ever seen any episode of it before) and there's an autistic contestant named Eva who opened up to a fireman named Joe early on in the season about having support needs. She tells him that if she has a meltdown she might need him to squeeze her hands and help her get grounded. He takes this ask very seriously and at one point in the show, Joe—now shuffled onto an opposing team—takes Eva's hands when she's very clearly having a panic attack and helps bring her back to well-being. Apparently, watching this scene between them is the only time the host has ever cried in the series.

Babe, I just needed you to be Joe, I said to Char after that whole meltdown fight thing we had where I ran. I think I just needed a hug. She nodded and hugged me, but also tried to explain that I need some more tools because she can't always be Joe. We were both Eva in that moment, she'd said, so I went online and ordered *The Couple's Autism Workbook.* Its author is British, I think, and it has an illustration on the cover of a brain and a heart sitting in high-back chairs, each reading a book illustrated with a heart and a brain respectively.

I don't wish for self-control, I wish for kindness, I realize. To be met, by myself and by others, with gentleness.

Today I checked things off the large list of what it calls "overwhelming sensations" in order to learn about myself more. They have a ranking system that's numbered 1–10 of discomfort. I put vacuum sounds as a 10, along with the texture of meat and a fridge-running sound, a 2 are dogs barking and a 7 is someone chewing. I also have a 10 for being interrupted and a 7 for being in the sun, an obvious 15 is fluorescent lighting, another 10 is using numbers, which is funny. The author encourages readers to de-escalate when these things are happening in too quick a succession—play, breathe, distract, swim, shower, rest, receive a hug.

"No one teaches us what to do with a pain that never stops," the author David Morris writes in *The Culture of Pain*, but that's not true, you taught me what to do. You tried to have us live in a calm world with low lighting and quiet reading time, life bucked us off this, but I do remember your trying. You and Grammy taught me that sitting by the sea does a lot for this and that going out to run errands at 11 a.m. is a good time and staying out of the heat is important but also so is getting sun, and doing anything after

3 p.m. will probably lead to being sick with overwhelm because of the business of the day, which whips up around then in terms of traffic and people. I'm talking about a meld of bodymind pain here (another Linklater word), because how could the "body" be separate from the "mind" really? It's actually all one organ: a bodymind.

You and Grammy had your own sheet music to accompany this experience that you gave to me. I play it. The other part is that it showed up in you both as a stoic thing. Morris writes about that too, how a person's reaction to pain is socio-cultural as well as physical and theological. He cites Mark Zborowski, a researcher who published a book in 1969 called *People in Pain,* in which he recounts that Irish people, for example, reported needing to "take" their pain like it was a punch.

"The strikingly homogeneous behavior within each group was matched at times by other similarities that cut across ethnic lines," Zborowski writes. "For example, regardless of ethnic origin, many patients from lower social classes similarly interpreted pain as a threat of unemployment and financial ruin… They gave every pain a safe or nonfatal explanation..."

I remember you doing that, telling yourself any illness was just stress because missing work was never an option. Job loss was your principal concern always. It was snow on the screen of your mind and mine. I learned to act a certain way and write a certain way, making sure no detail about you ever slipped through that would threaten your work. It was one of the only direct asks you ever made of me about my writing.

I wish I could have known more about myself while you were alive. My fantasy is that I could have realized all this like even a month before your death, brought you this autism workbook, helped you realize it, fixed it all. I had pictured such a different future for us, but I have to relent and let your death be the truth of it.

I hear clear laughter now from outside, which happens often from the trap shacks. I usually pause and look off into thin, slanted sunlight toward the sound. I'm doing it now, thinking about Barthes.

"As soon as someone dies, frenzied construction of the future (shifting furniture, etc.): futuromania," Barthes writes. I try to rearrange my whole imagined life, envisioning a new future from this house I built for us.

"Saving," Solnit writes, of the desire to protect or control outcomes, "imagines an extraction from the dangerous, unstable, ever-changing process called life on earth. But life is never so tidy and final. Only death is."

Recently, I read Olivia Laing's book *The Garden Against Time: In Search of a Common Paradise*:

"I'd got the relationship between death and the garden all wrong. I'd somehow internalised the idea that a good garden is a deathless garden, in a state of continuous perfection, even as I'd rejected the notion of it as a sealed sanctuary, a refuge from the outside world with its plagues and wars. But neither of those things were possible. The garden was always engaged in a dance with death... So many of our most ecologically deleterious behaviours are to do with refusing impermanence and decay, insisting on summer all the time."

I think often now that a garden is a place to practice watching expressions of life die.

* * *

There's a trail to the sea here with roots elbowing out of the path and right now I could fall through into a rich mud. It crunches with ice and rocks. I've never liked the spring until now. I saw ripples in the vernal pool and was filled with shame when I realized I put the house within a hundred feet of it. When I built the house, we were in a drought. I didn't expect to find, the next year, deep V's of water marbling out the terrain on either side of it and a large pool that ducks skidded into. All the way into June, I'd find tangles of baby ribbon snakes under pots, hefty dragonflies dead in cups of water I'd left out accidently, thin-fingered blood-orange newts in the bathroom, and all the frogs. At first, this seemed very ugly, the wet alders in mud, and all the swamp maples, leaning in like around a fire. But the chorus at night in June is incredible and I'd never seen so many songbirds as last year and we don't have mosquitoes, because the frogs eat them all. I saw a bobcat with its stub tail haunched and hunting wood frogs the other day. You could have sat on our deck in a lawn chair and I could have bought you Diet Coke and we could have watched the spotted salamander tadpoles skating around.

We both struggled to leave our houses, maybe equally.

I am still picturing a dream where our bodyminds have fewer needs. I want to stop dreaming about this and be down for the disappointment: the breakdown of our communication, the breakdowns of our bodies… all of it.

"The eventual disappointment of hope is not a reason to forsake it," writes José Esteban Muñoz in *Cruising Utopia*.

I had no idea before writing this book that the word "utopia" comes from an imaginary island society in a book of fiction written by Thomas More and published 1516, from the Greek *ou-topos*, "no place" or "nowhere," which is satire. Utopia is "nowhere." This origin of the word, as writers like Susan Bruce point out in her *Utopian Justifications: More's Utopia, Settler Colonialism, and Contemporary Ecocritical Concerns*, comes from More's fictional world "built on the exploitation of the environment and the ones outside of their utopian society." Apparently, More's *Utopia* was a parody of narratives of sea-voyage colonization and attempts to show the absurdity and harm of colonial manifest destiny.

"This was no island at first, but a part of the continent. Utopus, that conquered it... brought the rude and uncivilised inhabitants into such a good government, and to that measure of politeness, that they now far excel all the rest of mankind," More writes of the fictional founder of Utopia.

I still often find myself only able to be happy if everything goes right, if there's no smell in the wall from a dead mouse, or if the dogs get along, if the light is good, the temperature is perfect, if the right things are happening everywhere.

Through Rebecca Solnit, I find Eduardo Galeano's quote about the unattainability of all this: "Utopia is on the horizon. I move two steps closer; it moves two steps further away. I walk ten steps and the horizon runs ten steps further. No matter how far I walk, I will never reach it. What is utopia for? For that: it serves to walk."

Right now, your ashes are facing out the window in my living room. I've hung your orange angel ornament you'd made off this urn I got on Etsy. It's perforated like a church incense burner for light to come in, which feels important to me. Your ashes are still in their original plastic bag because I had no idea what to do with them. Pour them out of that somehow? This urn looks out at your bird feeder and the copper-roof birdhouse I got you on that trip in 2008. I don't even know if you wanted to be ashes. I am continually startled by your absence. My body reacts before my consciousness can catch up.

"How am I going to manage to live here all alone?" Barthes writes of his mother.

* * *

I walk the old logging road on the land where I live and I know that I don't understand death at all. I have no idea where you went. I walk this trail almost every day. I try to make it to the ridge, which is halfway to the cove. This is the highest point on the peninsula and covered in so many different kinds of mosses that fan out across it. The air thins and that's obvious. There were purple mushrooms all last year around the oak at the top. I've seen a buck coming out of the balsams and I've also seen a bunny carcass with almost everything gone but its feet. I often turn back here but if I keep going, it's another mile and a half and then the sea. From this point on, the forest is denser, so there's shocking things along the path, like large trees blown down in wind with root balls taller than a garage and coyotes.

I wanted to walk with you here so badly, like we'd done at Little Long Pond. Lately, I've decided that we can, and I open my hand to hold yours as I go into the opening of the woods. I feel a tingling in my palm that I identify as you, and I keep my hand open like that, sometimes for hours.

"The truth about mourning is quite simple: now *maman* is dead, I am faced with death (nothing any longer separates me from it except time)," Barthes writes.

His mom died in 1977 and only a few years later, on February 25, 1980, he was knocked down by the driver of a laundry van while walking home through Paris. One month later, on March 26, he died from the chest injuries he'd sustained.

The last two entries in *Mourning Diary* are from September in 1979, just six months before his car accident.

> September 1
> Suffering; impossibility of being comfortable anywhere; oppression, irritations and remorse one after the next, everything under the sign 'wretchedness of man,' used by Pascal.
>
> September 2
> Nap. Dream: *exactly* her smile.
> Dream: complete, successful, memory.

* * *

When it was time for this conversation, almost whispering to everyone, I said that you wanted to be buried at Little Long Pond. I said it louder when there was talk of having your service in a church. The scary image that wouldn't leave me alone was the idea of a big picture of you printed out and on an easel or something.

I was late to the service. We'd just gotten your ashes in a box from Fernald. It was just a straight-up box lined in that plastic. On our way to the island, we drove past a black lab loose in the road. We coaxed it into the car and brought it to the town hall, where they said they'd help.

If I was a musician, I'd play this part low and fast and building because I was now going to Little Long Pond without you. When we pulled up I was afraid there'd be no one, but instead Hank was directing traffic in the street while people coming to the memorial circled to look for parking. He'd also gotten a cellist to play. They were set up on the grass by the platform for dogs to jump into the water. The cellist had just stopped as I walked up and I watched him lower his bow into silence. Grandpa was sitting in the front row gently holding a stack of papers. Grammy was in a rainbow fleece, her eyes fixed on the ground. There was your portrait on an easel. The one from the family photos we'd taken in Dallas in like 2004 when you and Hank were trying to get back together and I was about to move away. It looked nothing like you. I sat next to Grandpa, in between him and Uncle Daniel. Daniel's wife squeezed my arm.

We've lost our dear mother, friend, and daughter in the loss of Marie, a priest said. He came from out of nowhere in slacks and a suitcoat. He continued, she was a very nice woman who had some troubles in her life. She liked to play tennis and was a little neurotic, he chuckled. She loved cleaning—it was an outlet for her OCD. He then read a Bible verse or two.

A monarch flitted by.

That's her, people whispered. That's her!

I didn't think it was.

Would anyone like to speak? the priest asked.

A dog splashed into the pond nearby. We could all see the ripples.

Grandpa raised his hand. He was so close I could hear the shift of his shirt as he lifted it.

Yes, sir, please, said the priest, gesturing him forward.

Hello everyone, Grandpa said. Thank you for coming out to celebrate the life of my daughter. He looked down at his paper. The sun glittered on the water behind him. People moved gently along the far side of the bank across from us. A sea breeze lifted, but mostly there was infinite warmth.

He looked back up. I am her proud father, he said.

A hush fell. Everybody knew you would have died to hear that.

I could hear my own heartbeat in my ears only because my mind was working overdrive to contain all the feelings. He said more about how brilliant you were and how full of love for God and for nature, how spiritual and special, and how he will miss you every moment for the rest of his life.

Grammy's hands were folded and calm. I wanted to hold her hand. I bit my lip instead. What was I supposed to be doing? I wanted to streak naked or yell at everyone. I wanted noise and chaos.

I stood up and said something I don't particularly remember and then I randomly had everyone say the serenity prayer.

Afterward, people lingered near the folding chairs like they were still waiting for something and nothing else happened. The cellist packed up. A few of the men stood in a loose circle near the mouth of the path.

I didn't want to talk to anyone because I seemed to want the wrong things. I wanted someone to say the word "suicide" out loud, so I said it to everyone. I said it and people dodged me. This felt like a resounding denial of your experience. It had been a lifetime since I'd felt this alone.

* * *

I keep this book around me now, it's by Alexandre Baril called *Undoing Suicidism.* Baril notes that people who have lived through the death of a loved one via suicide are called "survivors," the idea is that a person has survived another's suicide like a car crash, which Brail and others, including scholar and writer Bee Scherer, say is reductionist, focused on blaming the suicidal person and ignoring systems of oppression that lead to a life being unlivable.

"I maintain that we should consider abandoning the term 'suicide' altogether," writes Scherer. "From a social justice perspective, most 'suicides' i.e., self-completed deaths cannot be called 'self-murder' i.e., 'suicides' properly: the illusion of the extent of individual agency that this loaded term carries only serves to absolve the system that creates the social injustice. Social injustice-induced and/or underpinned self-completed deaths are not really suicides; those self-completed deaths are, in fact, delayed, self-completed murders."

* * *

In our town, someone has installed a butterfly flower garden surrounding a decorated pole that's permanently on the corner. It's adorned with mementos related to the current season or, in the summer, the Fourth of July, alongside pictures of a teenager from the '90s mounted in a frame. This was the result of a tragic accident, a memorial for a neighborhood teen who was killed by a car. In town, there's a walk every year on her behalf, and the school is named after her. This walk happened very shortly after you died, and I remember watching this small parade of people walking past my house to the beach, where her mother, who started this memorial, has kept it up even twenty years on. This death was in the fold. All deaths aren't considered equal, particularly not ones considered a crime.

The philosopher Simon Critchley writes, in his analysis of the lives of Virginia Woolf and others, that suicide produces a "peculiar inversion of biography," where all of one's acts are read backward through the lens of the last moment.

Of course, I've been doing that nonstop, which was painful, but Baril writes that a lifetime of ideation is often absent from the narrative of a life, and needs to be drawn in after the fact, because suicidal people are denied the ability to speak about thoughts of killing themselves without the threat of institutionalization, job loss, and everything else. Thoughts are policed, he writes. As evidence of this, Baril notes that Critchley himself, in his book *Notes on Suicide*, felt obligated to reassure readers that he wasn't suicidal and not to worry about him. Baril says that he waited until tenure to write the book in which he outs himself as suicidal because he'd be somewhat protected against the institutional harms wielded against suicidal people, which had originally kept him from writing.

Baril coined the term "suicidism," which refers to structural violence against suicidal people, and explains that these contexts condemn "people to silence and push them to complete their suicide without having reached out to anyone." Brail goes on to write that "this is particularly true for [Black and Brown] racialized people and other marginalized groups, including queers and trans people and disabled/Mad people, for whom contact with a suicide hotline and the deployment of emergency services often involves high levels of violence by police officers and paramedics."

Instead, Baril praises the work of groups like DISCHARGED, a peer-to-peer support group for suicidal people (Deserving of Inclusion, Support, Community, Hope, Authenticity, Respect, Growth, Empathy, and Determination). The creators of DISCHARGED explain the purpose of the group like this:

"Peers will mindfully listen to each other's stories rather than trying to 'fix' or diagnose people. These groups are different to other suicide prevention initiatives because the goal is not to force someone to stay alive from moment to moment, the goal is to support someone in creating a meaningful life they want to live. Not killing one's self is simply a side effect of that."

* * *

I think I was particularly angry at your memorial because just a few days before I'd gotten a very simple email from the medical examiner with your toxicology report that had two PDFs attached to the email.

The toxicologist said that carbon monoxide poisoning was your cause of death and that you'd had only that in your system and some caffeine.

I clicked on the second PDF and it took me a second to understand what I was looking at. It was a photo of your ripped paper pad. A ballpoint pen was pictured lying on the pad under what you'd written. The tip of a police person's boot was in the frame.

It was called note.pdf.

I closed the PDF and opened it again. This was a clear photo of a note on your table at the bottom of the stairs.

Please contact

My daughter

emersonwhitney@icloud.com

[not my email]

My brother

[his number]

You'd written "please let" at the top of it all and crossed it out. Then, in your sweet, clear teacher handwriting, you wrote:

this is no ones fault.

I can not live alone anymore

with the demons I have

in my mind

I have tried

again and again

they just keep

coming back.

I'll never hold your note, because it was evidence, so it doesn't belong to me. It just lives in my Gmail as this picture.

At this point, my heartbreak was so supreme that I didn't cry at all. I just studied it. This was in contrast to the beginning, when I would cry at a coffee shop or the grocery like vomiting. I learned from this process that crying is the body's way to alert others to a need for help. I was also told by a friend that police didn't mention the note to me because I was a suspect until the investigation was closed, like how they asked me about the cat without telling me it was alive or not.

I've never heard you use the word "demon" in my life.

* * *

You know what we did after your memorial, Mom? The family scattered, but Char and I went to J&P's, to their haunted barn. It was the last week of October and this was my idea.

The barn was busy, but thinning out. It was decorated with hyper-real neon portraits of Dracula, a mummy, and other monsters, with corn husks and scattered fake severed limbs. Inside, there were black strips of plastic hanging from the ceiling, vignettes of knives stabbing skeletons, and black-light cartoon gravestones.

No one else was in the haunted house. No one was staffing it either.

A scream track played really faint as we walked through. A glowing banshee shot across us overhead. You had to step on a squeaky rat stuck to the floor on the way out.

Char and I kissed at the end. This was a "baby, your mom just killed herself with no blood, which was a kindness, and now we're surrounded by synthetic blood and black-light but just in a strange little barn at the edge of town" kind of kiss. Maybe you should cry, she said when we got in the truck. Maybe that would be a good idea?

I had my baby book with me because I'd just been carrying it around without opening it. The worn cover was so soft.

When we got back from J&P's there was no more family, no more food, no noise. I sat outside in a cold hammock. Tree limbs scattered light across my face. I pulled the baby book out of my bag and for the first time in my life, I opened it.

* * *

You notice EVERYTHING! you wrote.

> As a newborn, you easily noticed the light from a window. You watched our faces. You are very
>
> aware of sun and wind, none of which you like! We do our best to shield you from them both. Emerson, you seem to like the

sound the vacuum makes and sometimes I think you know my voice when I coo at you. You love music of any kind and will always fall asleep in my arms if I dance to music, we watch MTV and dance. I think you like my singing too. You love the clock in the living room and any noise I make with my mouth too.

Just this week I realized you actually do recognize us—when you see us for the first time when you wake up in the morning, you are all smiles—such a big warm grin, it melts our hearts! You don't smile like this for anyone else. As a matter of fact, this week you don't seem to like anyone else to look at you! You are giving us all your love. Thank you honey.
You very quickly discovered you could push pacifiers and barrettes in the VCR! Uh-oh we would say and uh-oh you would say after us! Due to a sore throat you discovered popsicles and how you loved those! You discovered one sunny day in July that you could push your own buggy! You could stop and explore something closer and even make a hushed giggle. You have been such a joy to be with. You are so responsive and so aware of everything. You have begun to really enjoy the car seat and the buggy. You love to take trips in either. This week we took you to the grocery and you played the whole time with a bag of marshmallows. You enjoy the library so much, you tuck your lower lip in and look at every book! Above all though, you like to be held—you fell asleep in my arms twice yesterday. I was the happiest, proudest mom in the world. You make me

so very happy. It is such a wonderful feeling—one that can't be duplicated.

Today sweetheart, I felt for the very first time what it felt like for you to enjoy yourself without me—oh the emotions that stirred inside me—you and mommy and Hank were at a fair in Westport on a beautiful Friday evening. We bought our tickets and you first rode the merry go round with Hank. We waved each time you passed while Hank held you. Then you rode your very first alone. You were in your own car with a steering wheel and a horn! You gave the man your ticket and off you went! My pain and sadness to sheer joy—that three minute fair ride. Oh how I cried, my baby was on her own! I could never forget the look on your face, the joy you felt, the freedom, my loss. I don't know what is to come honey, but I hope we are always close, closer than close, it's my prayer.

* * *

I stopped reading and looked up and Char was standing next to me. I had tears streaming down my face and the sun was just reaching over to the west but was streaking everything pink. I put the book face down in my lap and turned toward the house. It had careful pine siding that would eventually go gray like a barn and big glass doors and windows facing us. I could see all of Char's cute lamps making warm light across her art on the walls. Our couches and chairs were turned toward each other and the dogs were little outlines inside watching us. I'd felt forever like I was looking into the windows of someone else's life. I stood up. Char held out her hand to lead us back inside.

* * *

Want to go to the Blue Hill Fair? She was asking me a few days later. I'd gone into the house with her and hadn't left for days. Everybody's wanting us to go, she was saying

My friends were trying to keep me busy because I was losing it.

Let's try it, she said, right?

I'd just read the thing about the fair that you wrote in the baby book, so I was like, okay, sure, actually yes.

You and I had never gone together but you always wanted to go. I kept trying to catch sight of you in the crowd around the midway with that blinking Moby-Dick ride and all the fair food you liked and the farm animals. The people in Grundens and waders and thick farm boots mixed with some tourists but not many. We all sunk into the mud. I realized out there that I was too far from home, off island and out of sight of the mountains.

You make this joke in the baby book that I wanted you and Hank to get me a bright red notebook at a library sale and I begged so you guys got it for me. I sat down with it when we got home, found a pen, opened it, and started scribbling: look, I'm writing in my diarrhea, I'd said.

I thought about this as we walked around the fair and I laughed to myself, remembering your voice in my head. I was terrified to lose your voice. I didn't even stifle my laugh because of my state, and no one bothered to point it out either.

I was standing with Char and our group of friends in the lemonade line when someone with a bleach-blond ponytail, tortoise-shell glasses, and a pink flannel passed by in front of me. The person caught my breath.

I could feel you. I don't know how else to say it. The sense I have of you was there, warm and funny and kind, a pink feeling.

As I was experiencing this lightness of seeing almost you, I was struck, suddenly, by the idea that I had been thinking of things all wrong. If I believed your death was caused by ableism, which I did, seeing myself as overly responsible or capable of saving you was a way for this same ableism to thrive—it was living in me as a mother lode of shame. What if you were wanting me to just be your child? Maybe that's why you didn't call me for help. Maybe you didn't want me to build you a house and fix it all. Maybe you didn't want me to keep you alive. I wanted to more than anything at all ever, but believing I could is denying you agency and respect, really. The person resembling you disappeared into the throng of fairgoers walking into the *Charlotte's Web* exhibit, which was perfect because you loved *Charlotte's Web*. Char brought me my lemonade and leaned against me for a second.

I wanted to tell you about this:

I've recently begun talking to people about having ADHD and autism–AuDHD–EDS, and all those acronyms and for some reason it's going well. In some ways, it still feels wrong because those are these deeply imperfect labels, but I like what Grant Bruno writes about neurodivergence in "Decolonizing Autism Research," saying that Eugen Bleuler coined the term "autism" to describe a "withdrawal into one's inner world." We both have the gift of rich inner worlds, but together we didn't have to withdraw from each other. You know? We could be in these states together. Bruno writes that Haudenosaunee elders at Six Nations of the Grand River attest to the fact that understanding, gratitude, and acceptance for people who exhibit traits now called autistic or neurodivergent have been practiced for hundreds of years and likely since time immemorial.

I'd never experienced gratitude for these traits outside our family. I miss sharing this with you with a longing that feels unfathomable. Grieving you and our shared world, I've suddenly become too weak, or maybe too strong, to hide this want.

Yesterday, I got upset with myself about how I'd done something wrong with our gray-water system outside in the cold. Char came to try and help. I'd taken off my hat and tossed it onto the driveway. She didn't get angry with me or hurry me or anything. She set down whatever was in her hands and went to hug me. She made a joke about me being mad, which was fun, and said, are you going to run around with your pants falling down again? Everything's okay, it's just hoses. It's not a big deal. We're still going to have a great day. She hugged me and we rocked back and forth.

Birds bounced on the wires overhead and the mountains in the distance turned purple.

I was back in my body.

This is your gift to me, Mom.

* * *

You and I always joked about having a tendency toward an "all or nothing" mindset. A person at the grocery looked at me wrong, so I'm never leaving the house again, type of thing. When I first started using a wheelchair, I wanted a manual one because I thought it would make me look cool. I was picturing myself seen by some imagined nondisabled person—a harder-to-use chair signaled athlete, I thought. I refused to listen to people telling me I'd be much happier in something electric.

I'm talking about internalized ableism, I guess. My tangle of mobility and neurodivergent support needs have made me feel a lot of shame, I believe we shared this.

At the Blue Hill Fair, in my deepest grief, I was shameless. I held nothing back. I used a random arm crutch half the time and dropped it in the mud when I felt like leaving it behind. I had my baby book with me in a bag along with that green stuffed bear you'd made with one short and one long leg. I was hyperverbal and everyone let me be. Afterward, I didn't ruminate on anything I'd said and I didn't worry that anyone disliked me. This felt breezy. The violence of grieving you was the first time I really couldn't help but surrender all control and show myself. I'd spent so much of my life trying to escape embarrassment, which meant I was living with a fear of doing anything that made me seem not-able, particularly since I was a teen. In this way, ableism was a wedge between us. I kept any care you offered me at arm's length.

Lately, I've shifted to using a power scooter I found on Marketplace at work, and often use nothing at all unless it's going to be a long day somewhere. Right now, my manual chair, with its nice opalescent frame, is in the attic with its wheels off, leaned against all your Tupperwares full of old papers. Until I can get a power attachment, it's too hard to use, honestly. The mobility scooter is outside where it's not supposed to be, in case it rains, my empty iced-matcha cup from this morning is getting sticky in the basket, sandy loam coating the footrest from the dust of our driveway.

* * *

In July 2004, when I was seventeen, you wrote in the baby book, *hi my baby,*

> My wonderful Emerson, the day before yesterday you left for college… what a hole in my heart your leaving created. I just keep reminding myself how ready I know you are for this step (except I am really regretting that we left your driving lessons to Hank! I wish you had driven more) I know you are going to love college and that college will love you! I know this isn't your first choice, but I'm hopeful now you can at least just focus on reading and writing and not have much more math! We spent a great week together "packing" and watching old movies and we even stitched together. Remember fondu at the melting pot? :) ! We shared memories we treasured and our favorite was the snow drive to UCONN, Sturbridge village, and the pumpkin farm. It feels so different for a mom when your baby goes to college—so final. I can't go in your room yet to box your things without crying. I slept last night in your gray fleece. I hold a soft friend of yours to fall asleep. Remember the beautiful statue we bought for the garden before you left? She is a treasure. But nothing like the treasure you are. We have had more than our share of "snags" between us during our lives thus far… my fault

entirely. I tried the best I could to stay a family with traditions and love and laughter at the "little things." I know I never gave you all you wanted or deserved and I am sorry. Maybe this can be a new beginning for us. I need you in my life honey. I miss when we were close. I miss you terribly now. But I want you to be happy! Remember how your hermit crab lost its claw on the way to the airport? I am glad he stayed here. He reminds me of you and I get to take care of him until you come home again. I miss your smile and your laugh and your confident step. I even miss your room all strewn about with dirty socks! Your whole room at times would smell like one big sock! I miss taking you to school—watching you walk away with so many bags on your shoulder! I miss your junky giant bags and your sandals—I miss going to Gap and Starbucks. I miss you so much Emerson. My heart aches for all the things we didn't do. Please, please lets make some new memories just you and I. Please give me a chance to be a positive, reliable, loving force in your life. I need you Emerson. I love you Emerson.

* * *

You ended the baby book with an entry from after I left home.

My sweetie, you said.

I am writing about a "silly" incident that didn't feel so silly to me… do you remember fainting at the doctor's office when you got your before college physical? I was so worried especially when you started to cry. Oh how your tears broke my heart. You were afraid and I treasure the fact that you shared your fear with me. I loved hugging you and comforting you. You helped me feel like your mom one more time before you left for college. Thank you honey. You have already left for school and the house and my heart are lonelier now and they probably always will be… we have already shared three or four great phone calls. We seem closer, more personal when we talk now. I love that! You can count on me sweetie to be a great long-distance mommy. I want to talk to you, mail "sillies" to you, show you my love consistently so you know how much you are missed. I love you, mom.

The very last page of the book is a maple leaf glued in and my baby hand and footprints in splotchy red ink. The caption is: This leaf is from a late September walk your grandmother took you on—was perhaps the first buggy ride you seemed to enjoy! Grammy covered your buggy with an afghan to shield you from the sun and you loved that. You were off!!

* * *

Mom, every single day, I think we should have had a parade for you—the world should have a parade for you—with foghorns and giant puppets of chickadees and squirrels and flowers, boats and people in boots and yellow sou'westers waving from the shore.

I do wish we'd have been able to laugh about it all, you know?

I know it felt too bad at first but remember laughing so much about jail and Martha Stewart? We could have laughed about whatever happened at Walmart. Grammy and I made jokes just the other day about how the Michaels in Bangor now has a self-checkout, saying, well, Mom would have gotten a kick out of that...

I'm so desperately sorry you were scared even for a second.

This is what I think about most.

* * *

Now, we've moved almost all the elements of your yard to my yard. Your rainbow windmills, that copper birdhouse, your little rock sculptures, painted porcelain mushrooms, five bird feeders, your two plastic fountains with multicolored marbles in them. I had to leave behind that weeping cherry tree that you and I planted together and the moss. I have your coffeepot, too, with your last coffee grounds in the filter ready to go for the morning. I keep it like that thinking someday I'll drink it.

This year, it's been wild. Since December, winter storms have moved inland in waves. They ate the docks, swallowed the street. The wind knocked out power for weeks. Your little rock bench hulked there. The wind howled. The water kept rising. I stayed in for a long time and hung up all your art. The experimental embroidery you were doing of the island is framed in the living room with its loops and careful colors in circles and twists. Your needles are still in the blue felt background that you were using for water, ready to go. We framed it with them in there. The house I built is strong around it.

As soon as the storms stopped, we stepped out of the house onto the deck. We could hear someone yelling *shit* nearby and clanging lobster traps mingling with the metal smell of a barrel fire. At least ten chickadees were at your feeder out front, going chickadeedeedee in the brightest winter light you can imagine, a red squirrel squat below it waiting for seeds to drop. Char and I sat in the steps out front and she put her head on my shoulder. Her tattoo that says BONNE CHANCE looked up at me from just above the notch of her neck.

* * *

I couldn't stay in the house anymore after that long freeze, so I walked the logging road through thick snow to the ridge. It was my first walk on the trail here since December. I wore a balaclava. I left the dogs at home and they watched me leave. At the very top of the ridge, coyote tracks started, just about the place where I'd found the dead rabbit, blood spattered across the snow. The thing I want to tell you about most is that after a certain point, the coyote tracks didn't stop or veer away like they usually do, they kept up with me. The tracks and I went together past that die-off of a whole lifetime of spruce on the ridge, we went down the ridge into the cedars and I started to get scared. No one would hear if I called. The coyote prints didn't leave the trail even once. How hungry would I be if I was a coyote with everything iced up like this? I thought about turning back. I really did. But I stayed with it. When I got down the ridge to the most tremendous cedar, the biggest one that had survived the two rounds of clear-cutting, the towering tree was surrounded by hooves of all sizes making rings in the snow and pee sprinkled on radiant ice.

This is the densest part of the forest. The coyote tracks circled and I wondered if a deer had been killed.

In the summer, these grasses are full of thick bees, now it's bunny tracks mostly and knee-deep snow. I waded further out toward the sea. I aimed toward the place where the smelt run was quiet with snow. The ice on it made every single color in sunlight.

My body stumbled toward the water because I'd been missing the ocean and because the snow was so thick and also because I got tired. The cove looked perfect for seals with ice chunks that crunched and seagulls slipping around.

I was suddenly sure that I'd die here on this island. I will also wake up when I die like I do from so many dreams and say, damn, I spent all night looking for my keys. Why was I so worried?

I'll die here just like you did, I thought as I stood out there, looking past the bay and toward your house—maybe even on my way back, who knows.

I paused and took a big breath, which I never do, just to feel it.

ACKNOWLEDGMENTS

Thank you to my wife, Charline—everything's better together. To my grandparents, who have loved me so well for my whole life, I am infinitely grateful for you. To my brothers and Hank, I'm glad we get to keep loving Mom together. Whit! Thank you for caring for me so much and being my buddy. To all my buddies near and far who saw me through this, I love you! And my beaux parents Gigi and Christian, merci pour toute votre gentillesse et votre soutien!

Huge thanks to Tim Wojcik, who supported me at every turn. Thank you from the bottom of my heart to Amanda Uhle, for your unwavering dedication to seeing my work in the world, to Claire Boyle, whose wisdom and care made this book what it is, thank you for your patience and presence with this project, which is my heart, and to Dave Eggers for all the love and kindness.

To all those who helped: Maggie Nelson, Clay Kerrigan, Jamila Cornick, Clay River, Olivia Spring and *SICK* magazine, August Sender, Pete Franzen, Grammy and Grandpa, my dad and sisters, Carrie Ashley Hill, Scott, Debbie and Carole.

Rest in Power Lilac Vylette Maldonado and Miss Major Griffin-Gracy.

Niawen'kó:wa to Bear Fox and her "Sky World Song," which brought me so much peace.

This book is written in loving memory of both my mother and father, who began their afterlives in 2022 and 2025 respectively. Thank you, Mom and Dad, for taking me everywhere as a baby, and especially to the beach.

To protect the identities of those in the text, names in *O Mother* have been changed and identifying details have been altered. *O Mother* was written via recollection and reflection, and all inaccuracies are purposely left uncorrected.

Baby book entries and other archival material from my mom are published verbatim with the purpose of expressing her voice, minus identifying details. Any errors are also left uncorrected.

ABOUT THE AUTHOR

Emerson Whitney is the author of the critically acclaimed memoirs *Daddy Boy* (McSweeney's, 2023) and *Heaven* (McSweeney's, 2020). Their work has appeared in *The Paris Review*, *New York* magazine, *The Los Angeles Review of Books*, and elsewhere. The recipient of the Maine Writers & Publishers Award for Memoir in 2024, Emerson is grateful to live Downeast.